CHILD
OF MANY COLORS

CHILD
OF MANY COLORS

Stories of LDS Transracial Adoption

Compiled by

Shannon Guymon

CFI
Springville, Utah

Editor's Note: Unless otherwise captioned, the photographs in this book are meant to represent transracial families and children in general and do not necessarily depict the specific families mentioned herein.

ISBN 13: 978-1-59955-325-2

Published by CFI, an imprint of Cedar Fort, Inc., 2373 W. 700 S., Springville, UT 84663
Distributed by Cedar Fort, Inc., www.cedarfort.com

LIBRARY OF CONGRESS CATALOGING-IN-PUBLICATION DATA

Guymon, Shannon, 1972-
  Child of many colors : stories of transracial adoption / Shannon Guymon.
    p. cm.
  ISBN 978-1-59955-325-2
  1. Interracial adoption--Anecdotes. 2. Adoption--Religious
aspects--Church of Jesus Christ of Latter-day Saints. I. Title.

  HV875.6.G89 2010
  332.734092'2--dc22

                    2009045369

Cover design by Jen Boss
Cover design © 2010 by Lyle Mortimer
Cover photographs (clockwise from upper left): stock photography, Kaleb Guymon (by Kathy Tenney), stock photography, the Guymon family (by Kathy Tenney)
Interior photographs courtesy Matt Peterson (used by permission), except photo of Ruby Guymon on p. 96 and Guymon family on p. 101
Edited and typeset by Heidi Doxey

Printed in the United States of America

10 9 8 7 6 5 4 3 2 1

Printed on acid-free paper

Dedicated to

Kaleb and Ruby,
My beautiful, beautiful children.
You might not look like me,
but you are the best part of me.

and to
Skyler, Savannah, Jessica, and Tucker,
My other beautiful children.
You sort of look like me, and you're
definitely the best part of me too.

Thanks for being such good brothers and sisters.

Be sure to check out these
fiction titles by Shannon Guymon

Taking Chances
Makeover
Soul Searching
Forever Friends
Justifiable Means
A Trusting Heart
Never Letting Go of Hope

and coming November 2010

The Broken Road

CONTENTS

Acknowledgments

This book could not have been written without the input and stories from the Yahoo! chat group for transracial families in Utah. I have learned so much from these amazing women who have sacrificed and who have put their children before themselves. These women are amazing. These women are inspiring. These women are tough! They stand strong in the face of prejudice without flinching. They're stared at, and they're categorized, and they're judged unkindly sometimes, but they can take it. Because they're moms.

These moms love their kids more than anything. They've given up the finer things in life and have done without to bring their children home. They've spent hours and hours learning how to make sure their daughter's hair looks just right, so she can stand proud in a world that judges on appearances. They learn all they can about a different culture so they can teach their children about their heritage. And most important, they teach their children that they are cherished sons and daughters of God. These moms are the best moms in the world, and this book is a celebration of their strength, courage, and love.

PREFACE

This book started out as a love letter to my children and then grew into a love letter to all of the beautiful black children adopted into transracial families. I remember when I first brought my son Kaleb home from the hospital. I looked all over the place for a book that he could relate to—a book that would help him understand that while he is unique, he's not so different either. There are many amazing books out there on adoption, but not many books for black children who are adopted by white parents. And there are even fewer books about transracial families that testify of the eternal nature of families. Even though this isn't exactly a children's book, it is a book that my kids can pick up and open to see pictures of families just like theirs.

I know without a doubt that I was meant to be a mother to my two adopted children. I know it the same way I know I was meant to be a mother to my biological children. It's written in my soul. I've known these children forever. As you read my story of adoption and all of the other adoption stories in this book, you'll start to see patterns. Not only were these children meant to be in the homes they came to, but Heavenly Father went to a lot of trouble to make sure they got where they were supposed to be. Heavenly Father truly is a God of miracles, and every story in this book will show you how he took impossible, complex, hopeless situations and orchestrated events to bring joy, happiness, and completion to our families.

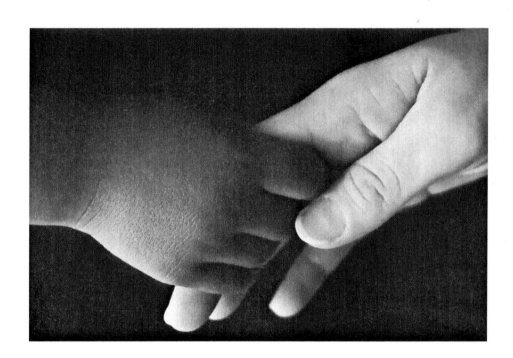

1

MATT & SHANNON GUYMON'S STORY

I believe I have come to better understand that the Lord's tender mercies are the very personal and individualized blessings, strength, protection, assurances, guidance, loving-kindnesses, consolation, support, and spiritual gifts which we receive from and because of and through the Lord Jesus Christ. Truly, the Lord suits "his mercies according to the conditions of the children of men" (D&C 46:15). . . . We should not underestimate or overlook the power of the Lord's tender mercies. The simpleness, the sweetness, and the constancy of the tender mercies of the Lord will do much to fortify and protect us in the troubled times in which we do now and will yet live. When words cannot provide the solace we need or express the joy we feel, when it is simply futile to attempt to explain that which is unexplainable, when logic and reason cannot yield adequate understanding about the injustices and inequities of life, when mortal experience and evaluation are insufficient to produce a desired outcome, and when it seems that perhaps we are so totally alone, truly we are blessed by the tender mercies of the Lord and made mighty even unto the power of deliverance (see 1 Nephi 1:20).

—*Elder David A. Bednar*[1]

From a young age, I knew, deep in my bones, that color was just part of a person. I knew with all my heart that my best friend, Sean, was the coolest girl in the world. Yes, she was black, but in my eyes, that only made her even more special. I didn't know anything about Martin Luther King Jr. or Rosa Parks. I just knew we were two little girls who happened to be happiest when we were together.

From this friendship, I developed an acceptance for people who weren't like me and a love for black people especially. We moved away when I was six, and I didn't see Sean again until I was in my late twenties.

One memory I treasure is of being twelve years old and babysitting for some people in our church who were black. They had the most gorgeous baby I'd ever seen. Her name was Asha, and I fell in love with her. Her face was so chubby and was the color of chocolate. Her eyes were a bright sparkly brown, and I loved to stroke her soft, curly hair. It was then that I thought, *Maybe someday I could have a baby like Asha.*

As we all know, life moves on and dreams are forgotten, and after getting married and having a few children, I had almost forgotten about Asha. But then I got pregnant with our son Justice. The whole time I was pregnant with Justice, I had morbid, apprehensive feelings that maybe something wasn't right. I'd had a little bleeding midway through the pregnancy, but everything else was pretty much normal. At least that's what the doctors kept telling me. But despite their assurances, I knew in my heart something wasn't right. So I turned to the Lord, and I pleaded for my son's life. I prayed day in and day out that my son would be born happy and healthy. But no matter how much I prayed, the bad feelings would never go away. Well, the last month of my pregnancy, I felt great physically. I started to think maybe all of the bad feelings were just hormones. Maybe I was wrong and everything would be okay.

On a gorgeous July morning, three weeks before my due date, my water broke. Matt and I smiled all the way to the hospital. This was it. Our family was finished. We would have two boys and two girls. The perfect family.

The nurses checked me in, got me settled in a delivery room, and started to hook me up to a monitoring machine. I remember watching the nurse's face closely as she studied the screen. Her smile disappeared quickly, and her face became tense. When she turned to look at me, I felt a dip in my stomach as if I had just fallen off the edge of a cliff. She said, "Let me go grab your doctor real quick. I'll be right back."

She and my doctor returned shortly with an ultrasound machine. He smiled calmly as he rubbed the gel across my stomach and then studied the screen intently. He rubbed geometrical patterns all across my stomach, but to no avail. There was no heartbeat. He finally put his hand down and turned to look at me. Then he said the three words I didn't want to hear: "I'm so sorry."

The next hour was more than a nightmare. Nightmares aren't so bad, really. You can always wake up from a nightmare. What do you call a nightmare that you can't wake up from? This was on a scale unknown to me before. I was immersed in despair—a sadness so heavy and a devastation so complete that I wondered how I could survive. My husband's pain was just as exquisite.

After I delivered the most beautiful, perfect child, the nurse somberly laid my son in my arms. It would be the only time I would get to hold my son in this lifetime. I'd never had experience with death before. I'd never held someone I loved with all my heart and known his spirit was already gone. At that time we were blessed to have a grief counselor come in to help us through the next couple of hours. Her name was Heather, and she had been my visiting teacher many years before. Having Heavenly Father send me an old friend on the worst day of my life was truly a tender mercy. She helped us to bathe our child and wash him and dress him in a blessing outfit, donated for just such occasions as mine. She made molds of his hands and feet and took pictures for us to remember him by.

After she left, our bishop came in. He asked me if I would like to have a blessing. I nodded my head. The doctor couldn't tell me why my son had died, but I thought maybe Heavenly Father could. It was a beautiful blessing, and it gave me peace and comfort. In the blessing, our bishop told me that other children were meant for our family.

I remember thinking, *No way. No way will I ever go through pregnancy again.* I just couldn't. Soon after that, we had to say good-bye to our son, and after kissing his face one last time, we went home, where we had the heavy burden of telling our children that their little brother had died. I hadn't known that my pain could get any worse, but seeing my children's faces and feeling their disappointment and grief was almost unbearable. I don't know how we made it through those next two weeks, but I do know that if it hadn't been for the

Spirit, I wouldn't have made it at all. I know that Heavenly Father literally held me together.

One day a neighbor of mine, Cindi, took my kids for me so I could rest. Matt was at work, so I lay on the couch and tried to nap. I fell asleep for about an hour and when I woke up, I felt so incredibly warm, almost as if I had been held while I slept. The room was filled with the wonderful scent of flowers, and I knew then that an angel had come to comfort me. I was filled with the most amazing feelings of peace and comfort and love. And I knew that Heavenly Father loved me and was there for me.

The next year passed in shadows for me. There was no happiness for me; there was no sunshine. There was just enduring one day after the next. I smiled for my three children and loved them and treasured them, but happiness and joy were distant memories. My arms constantly ached to hold a baby. I remember sitting in church with my kids behind a family who had a young baby. My kids spent the whole time playing with the baby and smiling and laughing at her. Every few seconds it seemed, one of them would say, "Look, Mom! Look how pretty she is! Look, Mom! She smiled at me! Oh, Mom, I want a baby. Can't we have a baby?" And each time they said something, my heart would shatter all over again.

At this point, I went to my husband and said, "Well, I'm not willing to bear another child, but maybe we could become foster parents?" Matt readily agreed. We started the paperwork and started to hope. Maybe, just maybe, we could help out a family and still have a baby to love, even if it was for just a little while. That was at the beginning of summer. At the end of June I decided to take all of my kids to the pool one day. It was kind of an overcast day, but my kids needed the exercise, and I needed to get out of the house, so we drove down to the Lehi pool. We practically had the pool to ourselves, which was kind of fun. In this weather there was no fighting for chairs and no need to hide in the shade.

About a half hour after we arrived, I was lying back in my chair when Mike walked in. Mike used to be my brother-in-law. However, it had been a few years since his divorce and he had remarried. I immediately noticed the beautiful little girl he carried with him. I walked quickly over to the kiddie pool and sat across from him and his daughter. She was about a year and a half old and flat-out gorgeous. She had dark brown skin and the biggest afro puff ponytail I'd ever seen. I was enthralled. Mike couldn't help but notice me melt into a puddle of longing, so he told me how they came to adopt Olivia. I remember saying, "Oh, Mike. You are so lucky. I wish I could adopt a baby as beautiful as yours." He laughed and said, "Why don't you? You could have your own baby in just a few weeks."

I remember sitting there, kind of stunned. Everyone I'd talked to about adoption had always told me how complicated and expensive adoption was. It couldn't be the answer to our situation. Besides, we had already decided we were going to be foster parents. But that night, I called Mike's wife, Diana, who worked for an adoption agency, and she kindly told me how the process works. I couldn't help but get excited. Maybe this was our path. So I got the adoption application, I wrote a "Dear Birth Mom" letter, and I made a profile of our family with lots of pictures and stories of us. I turned it all in and started praying. I prayed that Heavenly Father would bless me with a baby. I prayed that he would bring joy and happiness back to our lives. I prayed and I prayed and I prayed.

Three weeks to the day that I had sat with Mike at the pool, I got a call from Diana, Mike's wife. She asked me if we preferred a boy or a girl. I wanted a girl after seeing Olivia and her glorious afro puff, but Matt insisted that we had to have a boy. So I told her we would only consider boys. That's when she got excited. They had a cute little birth mom who had gone into labor five weeks early, and she was about to have the baby any minute and hadn't picked a family yet. The birth mom said she just didn't feel right about any of the profiles she had already seen. Diana asked if she could show the birth mom our profile. I said, "Absolutely. Please do!"

After hanging up the phone, my heart started to race. I couldn't sit down, and I felt nervous and excited. This was my baby. I just knew this was my baby. Less than an hour later, I got a call from Diana, and she said, "Would you like to come to the hospital tomorrow to meet your new son?"

I couldn't believe it. I was so excited that I ran around the house crying and laughing as I tried to get everything ready. When we first turned in our papers, I had expected a six- to eight-month wait—minimum. Not in my wildest dreams could I have imagined a three-week wait. I called Matt and told him the good news, but he didn't believe me. He must have thought I'd finally lost it. But when he realized I was telling the truth, he became just as excited as I was.

The next day we drove up to Pioneer Valley Hospital and met our little birth mom. She was so sad, but she couldn't stop smiling at us. She took her son and put him in our arms. I cried with joy. I had spent the past year crying tears of grief, but on this day, joy filled my spirit as I held my son for the first time. This was the child that Heavenly Father had been talking about when he'd told me other children were meant for me.

As Matt and I signed the adoption papers at the hospital, we noticed that every date we filled in on the paperwork was July 9—the same day our son Justice had been born, exactly a year before. Heavenly Father had taken the saddest day of my life and turned it into one of the happiest. Heavenly Father will not leave us comfortless. He is our father, and we are his children, and we are important to him. Yes, we will suffer, and we will have trials, but he will never forsake us.

The next day, when we brought Kaleb home to our family, is a day I would like to relive over and over again. I don't think, lying in that hospital bed a year before, I could have ever dreamed that my pain could be taken away. But the day Kaleb came home, my heart was healed. My shattered soul was restored, and my arms were full.

Our story doesn't end there. The next year and a half passed quickly. Time flies when you're happy. But things never stay the same. I learned I was pregnant in June. For the next nine months I was flat-out terrified. My brother-in-law BJ, an ob-gyn, insisted on looking after me and the baby. But the one thing I had learned was that life and death are in the hands of the Lord. Even the best doctor in the world wouldn't be able to save my baby's life if that baby was meant for heaven. Every time I drove to the doctor's office for an appointment, I drove with tears on my cheeks. I just knew that when I got there BJ would search my stomach and not be able to find a heartbeat. Toward the end of the pregnancy, as I was busy sobbing my heart out on the freeway on my way to yet another checkup, I looked over and up into the sky and was shocked to see a rainbow. A perfect, small little rainbow, out in the middle of nowhere. I immediately felt a sense of peace and was comforted. This was my sign that my baby wouldn't be taken as Justice had been.

But I still insisted on being induced a couple weeks early. I didn't want to leave anything up to chance. As I was hooked up and given the pitocin drip, I started to relax. This was it. My baby would be fine and healthy. Everything would go well this time. But as the contractions started, I noticed on the printout that the baby's heartbeat went way down. It got so bad that every time I had a contraction, his heartbeat would stop all together. I was growing very upset by this time, and I kept saying to my husband over and over, "Do something! Do something!"

Then BJ came in and told me that they would have to do an emergency C-section. Within minutes, I was in the surgery room, being cut open. I remember holding my husband's hand and crying the entire time. I was scared to death of blood and knives, but if it meant saving my son's life, I'd do whatever it took. They finally pulled my son from my body and laid him on my chest. Beautiful, perfect, and alive! Tucker was finally here, and he was a miracle.

Finally, life was perfect. We had five beautiful children who were healthy and happy. We had a big family—bigger than I had ever planned on—but it was the family meant for me, and I was content.

After Tucker was about a year and a half old, Matt would start conversations by saying things like, "Do you think Kaleb needs a sibling that looks like him?" Or he'd be even more direct and say, "Maybe we should adopt just one more time." I would always roll my eyes and try to ignore him. Five kids were enough. Six kids would be downright insane. It was during this time that I was called to be a Primary teacher in my ward. When I was being set apart for my calling, the same bishop who had blessed me in the hospital when Justice was born told me in this blessing that my family would grow in size and number. I remember my breath catching as I felt the Spirit. *But how could the Lord want us to have more kids?* I thought. We already had so many!

I went home and kind of sighed. I just didn't know if I had it in me to be the mother of six kids. So I waited. I figured I'd put it off for as long as possible. But one spring day, as I was doing dishes, I looked out the window and saw the tiniest bird I had ever seen. She was hopping around as if she didn't know how to fly, and there were many larger birds of different species surrounding her. I was instantly worried for her safety. Where was this little bird's mother? Who would look out for her? As I sat and watched, the Spirit whispered to me that there was a beautiful little girl who needed someone to watch over her. There was a little girl coming soon who needed a mother who would protect her.

Hearing the Spirit's voice in my heart was all the motivation I needed. That same day I called my adoption agency and started the paperwork. If my little girl was coming, then I would do my part and be ready. I rushed as fast as I could to get all the paperwork done, and then I waited. And waited and waited! I had just assumed that everything would be as fast and easy as the first time we adopted. But no.

About six months later, we finally got a call from the agency that a cute little birth mom had picked our family. This was it! We were so excited. We talked to her on the phone, and Matt and I both fell in love with her bubbly personality. She was so excited and happy, even in her situation. We couldn't wait to meet her. She was due in about a week and a half and was scheduled to be induced. I ran to all the stores and bought everything a little girl needed. Pink everything! About a week went by, and I was in my car coming home from Target, where I had just purchased diapers and bottles, when I got a call on my cell phone from the agency owner. She first asked me where I was and, after learning that I was in my car, she kind of hesitated. I knew then that something bad was coming. She proceeded to tell me that our little birth mom had gone in that morning for her last doctors' appointment before the delivery. During the ultrasound, it was revealed that the baby had died.

I hung up the phone and drove home in a daze. *Not again. Not again. Please, not again.* But we had lost another baby. We would go to another baby's funeral. There's something especially heartbreaking about seeing a tiny casket placed in the ground. We hugged and comforted our little birth mom as best we could while our own hearts were breaking. We went home that day spiritually exhausted. Yet again, our children were disappointed and had to experience the grief of death. Yet again, we had to tell ward members and friends and relatives that the Lord had seen fit to keep this child. So after that, I was *done.* I told the adoption agency that maybe in a year or two we'd try again—maybe. I felt that I needed time to heal from this new heartbreak. They completely understood and were very kind.

Three weeks passed, and I got a phone call on my cell. I checked the caller ID and noticed it was the owner of the adoption agency. I let it go to voice mail. I just knew she was going to try and convince me to try again, and I didn't want to hear a pep talk. She couldn't possibly know what I was going through, and I didn't want to explain it to her. It wasn't until the next day that I finally listened to the message. It was kind of cryptic and mysterious. "Hi, Shannon. We have a very interesting situation here. Give me a call as soon as you can."

Well, I'm extremely curious by nature, so I couldn't just ignore that. I called just to see what was going on. What had happened was that they had a birth mom who wanted a completely closed adoption, so much so that she didn't want to even pick the adoptive family. She was leaving the choice of family up to the adoption agency. Everyone at the adoption agency wanted this baby to go to our family.

I did something really stupid. I said, "Let me think about it." I hung up and went and found my husband out in the yard. When I told him the situation, he looked pretty excited, but he left the decision up to me. My heart was in turmoil. Could I really try again? Could I really lay my heart out again, just to be crushed? I got in the car and drove to a beautiful, quiet look-out and prayed. The answer immediately came, *Of course you can! This is your baby!*

I called the adoption agency and told them I would be there at the hospital to get my daughter. The joy and excitement returned in waves. Even though our birth mom wanted a closed adoption, she still wanted us to be there for the birth. We were able to see our daughter born. Matt even cut the umbilical chord. As I held my daughter, moments after being born, the Spirit whispered to me once again. *This is your daughter.* This was the baby I was always meant to have. Here was the daughter I would look after and protect. Finally!

Now our family was complete. We brought our daughter home from the hospital two days later to five very excited children. Kaleb was the most excited, though. He kept saying, "Mom! Look at her eyes! They look like mine." "Dad! Look at her skin, she has brown skin just like me!" "Mom, Dad! This is my little sister."

People often ask, is it the same as having a biological child? Can you really love and connect to an adopted child the same way? I tell you that it's exactly the same. Why? Because the bond between a mother and child has nothing to do with eye color or hair color or freckles or any thing. It's a spiritual connection. And when you hold your child in your arms—a child that Heavenly Father has given you—you feel it. You can literally feel your soul connect to that baby.

And it's the most beautiful feeling in the world.

We have had many good people ask us why we adopted children from a different race. Won't the child resent us or resent his own race? Won't there be insurmountable problems? Isn't it too strange to adopt a child who doesn't look anything like you? All I can say is this. Motherhood transcends biology. Motherhood is a spiritual calling. At least it should be. The world will judge your children on everything they see on the outside—their skin, their clothes, their insecurities. It's your job to see their souls. It's your job to see the miracles that they are. And it's your job to make them see the miracles they are.

So when people, good people—even relatives and close friends—question our choices, we try and explain this to them. Our family doesn't look like everyone else's, but our family looks exactly the way Heavenly Father wants it to look. Now, years later, as I watch my children grow and develop into incredible people, I feel immensely grateful. Our path hasn't been easy, but it's the path that has led us to the children we were always meant to have.

2

COLIN & JEN'S STORY

God does nothing by chance but always by design as a loving Father. . . . William Law observed: "It is said that the very hairs of your head are all numbered. . . . If the smallest things we can conceive are declared to be under the divine direction, need we, or can we, be more plainly taught that the greatest things of life, such as the manner of our coming into the world, our parents, the time, and other circumstances of our birth and condition, are all according to the eternal purposes, direction, and appointment of Divine Providence?"

—Spencer W. Kimball[2]

The adoption seed was planted in my heart long before we actually adopted. Because of post-pregnancy complications, we began looking into adoption. At first I was convinced we would adopt blonde-haired, blue-eyed twin girls from Russia. We spent several years looking into different international programs. We researched countless agencies and adoption programs in almost every country. There were many tears of frustration (on my part—my husband was the patient one!) as we journeyed through confusion, trying to navigate our path to find our children. We finally decided to go forward with an agency and adopt from Guatemala. We were several thousands of dollars into the process when one day the Spirit prompted me very strongly. I can still remember where Colin and I were standing in our bedroom. I said to

11

him, "I think our children are in the United States!" Thus began more research as we turned away from international adoption and focused on domestic adoption.

One day we were at the mall, and we saw photos of children who were waiting to be adopted through the foster care system. We were drawn to a sibling group who were African-American and Caucasian. After pursuing this situation for a while, we felt it was not right, but we still felt drawn to the African-American culture. One day my visiting teacher was over, and she told me about her sister-in-law who had adopted African-American babies. She said the average wait was one to three months. This was it! We wanted babies, and we wanted them fast! Our youngest daughter was already five, and the gap was growing. We knew we wanted to adopt at least three babies of the same ethnicity so they could not only share adoption with each other but also their race.

We contacted the adoption agency and got our paperwork and home study completed. Colin made up a nickname for me, "Bulldozer Jen," because I plowed through as fast and hard as I could. We had about ten different birth mothers look at our profile before we were chosen. Each time a birth mother was going to be shown our profile, I would go to the temple and submit her name to the prayer role. Of course our hope was that we would be chosen, but in our hearts, we really did want her to make the correct decision for her baby, so we felt the extra prayers would help her, even if she didn't choose us.

It was an emotional roller coaster ride each time the agency called and said we hadn't been chosen. There were a lot of tears, again on my part—not on the part of my ever-patient husband. Finally, we got "the call." We had been picked by a birth mother. We were living out of state at the time, so we planned on heading to Utah, where the birth mother would be, to meet her and be there for the birth. As we were making the arrangements, the Holy Ghost prompted us to change our plans and head there a week early.

Later we were grateful that we had gone so early, because after we'd had a few days to spend with the birth mother and her other children, our baby was born early! It was an exciting day because it was our oldest son's birthday as well. Right after Ty was born, we knew there were problems. He was having difficulty breathing, so he had to stay in the NICU for three weeks. We moved into a hotel right across the street from the hospital for those three weeks. Luckily, Colin works from home, and our kids are home schooled. This made it easier for us to be flexible.

We visited Ty constantly. Here was our little newborn, only 5 lbs. and 2 oz., hooked up to all these huge life-sustaining machines. It was a hard time. We prayed a lot, submitted his name to the temple, and notified all our family members, requesting that they join us in a family fast. Soon after we fasted, Ty began to improve! From that point on, he got better and better until we were able to bring him home. He's been healthy and happy ever since.

When Ty was three months old, I felt prompted to check the adoption agency's website for "available situations," and I saw that twin girls were going to be born! We had talked about how neat it would be to end with twins, or at least "virtual twins"—two adopted children who were close in age. I still remember holding baby Ty in my lap at the computer, and with tears streaming down my face, I said to him, "Are those your sisters? Are your sisters coming?"

We contacted the agency and found out that this adoption situation was going to be a little complicated. The twins' birth mother wanted to keep the firstborn twin and raise her. However, if the birth mother was not able to continue to parent, she would place the first twin with us. We felt like this would be too difficult to have the twins separated and to not know if we would ever get the other sister. The caseworker asked if we would like to continue to be updated on this situation, and hesitantly I said, "Okay." We would find out later that this caseworker, along with other people at the agency, felt inspired that we were the right family for this situation, even though we didn't know it at the time.

About a month later, the agency called back to tell us this situation was still available. The Holy Ghost prompted us to pursue it, even though we had our reservations. We were selected immediately by the twins' birth mother, and again the Holy Ghost prompted us to head to Utah early. The birth mother was having signs of early labor, and one of the twins had a slower heartbeat than the other and didn't seem to be growing as well as her sister. Again we had the privilege of being able to spend a few days with the twins' birth mother before they were born. I was in the room during the delivery, which was a C-section. "Baby A" was delivered first, then "Baby B," the one who had been struggling. The birth mother and I marveled at how adorable they both were. It was an incredibly spiritual experience.

The twins were taken to the nursery, and Colin and I went into the nursery to visit our daughter, "Baby B," who we named Tiffany. I went over to see "Baby A," who the birth mother had named Shiloh. I looked at her cute little face and longed for her to be ours, but I had to set my mind and heart on the fact that this was not our daughter. I wasn't able to stay with her for very long because it was so hard.

Tiffany ended up in an incubator with a feeding tube for a week before we could take her home. Shiloh and her birth mother went home after a few days. We met once more at a park before we went back home. Again, it was hard not knowing if these twin sisters would ever know each other or have the opportunity to grow up together. It was completely beyond our control. The only thing we could do was to pray, fast, and put their names in the temple. Putting our trust in the Lord and having faith in his will was imperative for us so that we could move on. We had to trust and know that he was in control, even if we didn't understand. Now we had our virtual twins: Ty who was now four months and newborn Tiffany.

After three months we got a phone call from the birth mother. She was really struggling and things were difficult. We talked for quite awhile, and I hoped we would talk again soon. However, our contact with her didn't continue, much to our disappointment and worry. After another three months, we got the phone call we had been waiting for. The adoption agency called, and the woman on the line said, "She's ready." Immediately my heart began to pound, and I knew. I yelled to Colin, "We're getting Shiloh!" I was crying and shaking, and it was all so wonderful! The woman I spoke with at the agency had become a good friend after going through these experiences with us. She, Tiffany, and I got on a plane a few nights later and flew across the country to get my daughter.

It was so wonderful to see the twins' birth mother again, and of course, I was overjoyed to see Shiloh. I was struck by how beautiful she was! We went to a hotel to sign papers. We got the twins out of their car seats so they could play together and bond. In their six-month-old uncoordinated ways, they kissed each other's faces, hugged, laughed, babbled, and held hands. It seemed as though they recognized each other and were so happy to be together again! As

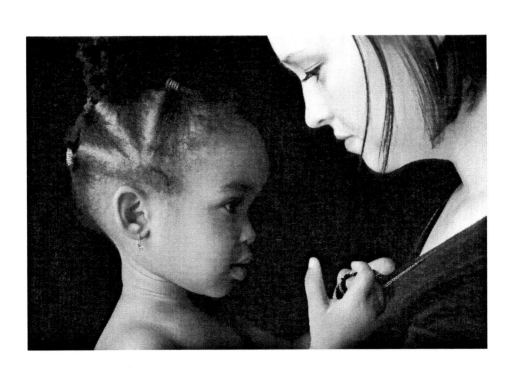

we said our good-byes, I felt intense sorrow for the birth mother. At the same time, I felt incredible joy and gratitude that Shiloh was now our daughter.

It's interesting how when we see other families like ours—white parents and black children—those families really stand out to us. When we are out and about, we must stand out like that to other people. We are just so busy with our six children (Ty, Tiff, and Shi are all now two!), that I frequently forget that we look "different."

If anyone ever asks, "Why did you choose to adopt black children?" my first response will probably be, "Well, why not!" The real answer to that question, though, is that we know how central the family is to God's plan for his children.[3] Our loving Heavenly Father knows where our children are. He leads and guides each of us by divine inspiration through our individual adoption journeys.

We are so grateful for our six children. Initially we wondered if we would feel the same intense love for and bond with our adopted children as we did for our biological children. The answer is, "Yes, we do!" Heavenly Father created each of our spirits, and whether our children are born from us or whether they are born from someone else, they are still our children. We are eternally grateful for the children Heavenly Father has blessed us with!

3

MIKE & MAUREEN'S STORY

Before we were born, . . . we made certain commitments . . . we agreed to come to this earth with great, rich, but different gifts . . . Hold your soul very still, and listen to the whisperings of the Holy Spirit. Follow the noble, intuitive feelings planted deep within your souls by Deity in the previous world.

—James E. Faust[4]

Our African-American son, Luke, joined our family in July 2005 through the miracle of adoption. However, our journey to transracial adoption began long before that, even though we didn't realize we were being prepared at the time.

I served a mission in my native England. Little did I know that I would have such a wonderful cultural experience serving in inner-city areas of London. I taught people from over thirty different countries, including Zambia, Uganda, Trinidad, Tanzania, Sierra Leone, Nigeria, the Ivory Coast, Jamaica, Kenya, Liberia, and Ghana. Fufu (a west African food) and jalaf rice literally became my staple diet there in London, and I learned phrases from Swahili, Yoruba, and other African languages. I really grew to love the African people while serving in an area called Peckham—or "Little Africa" to the locals.

My husband, Mike, was raised in Utah. We met while we were serving in the England London South Mission. He was my district leader in two different areas. There was no instant attraction; our relationship developed *after* our missions from a good friendship we had formed in the mission field. We do not believe that we could have met any other way. I finished my mission a month after Mike, in March 1996, and by the beginning of April that same year, I was on a plane to Utah to see him. It was a little nerve-wracking since we had only known each other in a formal way as missionaries. However, we soon realized through spending a few days together in Utah that there was more than a friendship there.

We became engaged in April 1996, and then I flew back to England to wait for the processing of my fiancée visa. We set the marriage date for the end of August, but there were several setbacks with the paperwork, and a few days before the marriage I still did not have my visa to enter the United States. But after a great deal of prayer and fasting, some divine intervention at the American Embassy in London, and a night spent sleeping in the passenger lounge at Heathrow Airport, I got my visa. We were married on August 21, 1996, in the Bountiful Temple. It was a wonderful day, and I really had no interest in whether the decorations or wedding colors matched up (a concern since everything was planned over the Atlantic); I was just happy and relieved to be there after so many challenges and setbacks.

We began our married life in Orem, living in Mike's father's basement. We soon moved to downtown Salt Lake City, so Mike could attend Salt Lake Community College. We started trying to expand our family as soon as we got health insurance coverage. Our son Jared was born in February 1998. We soon outgrew our one-bedroom apartment and moved to the University of Utah Student Village so that Mike could further his studies at the U of U.

When Jared reached the age of two, we started thinking of having another child. However, after about a year or so of trying, we sought medical advice and found out that there might be some infertility issues. Furthermore a physician told us in September 2003 that we'd had a biological miracle in Jared. It was then that we realized that our family would only expand further through adoption. At this point I was really committed to adoption, but it took over a year to get my husband on the same page. He finally agreed to let me fill out the paperwork for LDS Family Services (LDSFS), and we had our intake interview in mid-July 2004. I was very proactive in the adoption process and Mike was somewhat passive, which is apparently normal for adopting couples. We took the classes, completed our home study, and I even filled out the paperwork to register Mike with his Native American tribe.

I felt strongly that there was a baby boy who would come to our home in the summer of 2005, and this sense of urgency caused me to constantly be in finding mode. I knew that *I* had to find him. Since many adoptions are designated adoptions, and many birthparents prefer to place with a family recommended by a friend, LDSFS encouraged us to send out letters to family, friends, and acquaintances; I gave out in excess of a hundred pass-along cards and sent out letters all over the United States. I received three replies in response to these letters, and all three named an agency based in Utah that places mainly African-American children: Heart to Heart Adoptions.

I must say that I tend to be a bit of a sign-seeker—though not in a bad way, I might add—and I definitely saw this as a sign and an answer to prayer. By the end of May 2005, I felt so strongly that our son was out there, so I started checking in with Heart to Heart Adoptions. During the first week in June, I got a phone call from a lady there. She asked me if we were interested in adopting an African-American baby boy. The next day we got a phone call from LDSFS, saying that we were being strongly considered by a birth mother for a Native American adoption. It seemed like we had a dilemma on our hands; however, we were given a week or so to make a decision. After a great deal of fasting, prayer, and priesthood blessings, we knew that the African-American child was "our" son, even though the Native American child was what we had always visualized. A few weeks later, we went to the hospital and witnessed the birth of Luke. However, the greatest joy was being able to have the adoption finalized and have Luke sealed to our family six months later in the Ogden Temple.

Looking back, our lives have not gone exactly as we planned them, but the Lord has a way of preparing us and pointing us in the right direction if we will listen to the Spirit. Our lives have been enriched through transracial adoption. We have learned so much through the whole process. I am also amazed at all of the friendships I have gained through the process. Other people we met through visiting teaching and everyday life have also become part of our story; we have shaped each other's lives and helped facilitate getting children to the families where they were supposed to be. We wouldn't change it for anything! So why did I feel so strongly about getting Mike registered with his Mohawk Tribe? What was that all about? Looking back, I realize that filling out the paperwork was just occupational therapy—something to keep me busy until Luke was ready to come to our family.

4

PETE & ANGIE'S STORY

President Harold B. Lee gave some marvelous advice for modern pioneers. "Walk to the edge of the light, and perhaps a few steps into the darkness, and you will find that the light will appear and move ahead of you" (as quoted by Boyd K. Packer). We must walk by faith. That means stepping into the dark unknowns because we believe that Heavenly Father is awaiting us . . . .

—Bonnie D. Parkin[5]

I wanted to adopt my whole life. When I got married, I talked to my husband, Pete, about it, and he agreed that it would be a good thing to do one day. After we had our first three kids, we thought it was time to pursue adoption. We went through so much humiliation! We were living in Chicago at the time and couldn't believe the amount of resistance we received from different agencies. They questioned our motives because we already had children and told us that a birth mother would never pick our family because we already had kids. I couldn't believe it! We moved to Oklahoma with adoption still on our minds and in our hearts. There we got started with an agency, and a short time later we were told of a three-month-old little boy that needed a home. We prayed, we fasted, and I held that little boy. I thought for sure that he was our little boy, but he wasn't, and the situation ended up not working out. I was devastated. With the millions of children in this world without a family, and all of the kids in the foster care system with no families to call there own, I was shocked at how hard it was to adopt! I was so sad that the first situation didn't work out, and I was confused because we had both felt so good about it.

For the next four years, I tried really hard not to think about my dream of adopting. I was mad. Mad at the system and sad that it had to be so hard. In the meantime I got pregnant with twin boys and was busy taking care of our family. Our across-the-street neighbors at the time were African-American, and their youngest little girl was almost two. She was adorable, and every time I would talk to my neighbor and see her beautiful girls, there was something in my heart that knew—knew!—that my adoption dream wasn't over and that one day I would be the mommy of a beautiful brown baby with black curly hair.

A short time later, we moved to Utah. When the twins were almost two years old, I suddenly had a very strong feeling that we should try again to adopt. My husband and I prayed about it, fasted about it, and we went to the temple. We knew it was the right time, and we knew what Heavenly Father wanted us to do. I looked in the phone book and saw an agency ad that I felt good about. I called and over the next three months, we got all of our paperwork together and our background check and the home study done. The agencies here in Utah didn't discriminate against family size, and we were getting excited.

One day we got a call about a birth mom, and we were asked if we wanted our profile to be shown to her. Of course we did. She ended up picking our family to be the family of her soon-to-be-born baby boy. Preston was born two days later! Pete and I rushed to the store and bought a couple of bouquets of flowers for our birth mom and then went up to the nursery to wait for the caseworker to meet us there. I looked through the glass at all the babies. Then I saw him! I knew it was him. The Spirit bore such a strong witness to me that he was my son that it brought tears to my eyes.

We met with the caseworker, who said that our son's birth mom did want to meet us after all. I was so glad—I really wanted to meet her. Pete and I said a quick prayer together. I was so nervous. I kept thinking, *It could be anyone on the other side of that door!* We walked in and said our hellos. I gave his birth mom a hug. We gave her the flowers and started to get to know her a little bit. In the end, we talked with her for four hours! I felt the Spirit in that hospital room that day. When they wheeled in my new son and I picked him up, the warmest feeling came over me. I knew without a doubt that he was my boy.

A year later we felt like it was time to adopt again. We got all of our paperwork in order and prayed and fasted. We went to the temple. I painted our new baby's room pink; I knew it would be a girl. I ordered a dresser and washed all of my baby girl clothes. A short time later, we were picked by our daughter's birth mom. We got the opportunity to get to know her and our daughter's birth dad for five weeks before our baby was born. What a special experience that was, to have so much time to get to know them. Then our baby girl, Mylie, was born, and again the Spirit bore witness to me that this little girl was my daughter and that Heavenly Father had gotten her to us.

Six months later I had a dream. I dreamed about my youngest son. He was black, with really dark skin. I told Pete about my dream, and we decided to get our paperwork all ready to go. One day I was looking at our adoption agency's website, and they had a situation with the birth mom's name listed. When I saw her name and situation, I felt some kind of a connection. I called the agency and asked them to tell me a little bit more about her, but they said that she was looking for a family that didn't have any kids.

A few days passed, and I couldn't get her off my mind. I called again and told them that I already knew that she wasn't interested in a family like ours, but that I felt very strongly about her seeing our family profile. They agreed to put our profile in the pile that she was to see. That night we got a call from the caseworker, telling us that this birth mom wanted to have a phone conversation with us the next day. We were thrilled! We had a great talk on the phone, and she asked us to be the parents of her soon-to-be-born baby boy. Of course we said yes! We asked her why she picked us, especially because we knew that she wanted a family with no children. She said she felt a connection and knew we were the right family.

The next day we met her for dinner, and the day after that we got to meet her mom, who had come to support her daughter with this difficult decision. Two days later my baby Lakin was born. What a wonderful day! I got to watch him be born, and again I felt the Spirit in that hospital room after my new little son was born. I looked at his little face, and he was my boy!

My testimony has grown so much through the experience of adopting my three babies. The worth of a soul is great in the sight of God, and I *know* without a doubt that Heavenly Father has a plan for each one of us. He loves us all, and nothing is impossible for him. He brought our family together. He answers prayers. I don't believe in coincidence. Things happen for a reason—his reasons—and the three babies we adopted aren't just some random babies that needed a family. They are my kids, and Heavenly Father got them to me!

I have learned to listen better to the still, small voice. It is still, it is small, but if you listen, you will hear it. I have learned to trust my feelings, and I've learned that some things we feel with our hearts are truly whispers from the Holy Ghost, helping us to know what to do. Three of the greatest days of my life were the days we took each of my adopted babies to the temple. I watched my other children enter the sealing room, dressed in white, and seeing them confirmed what I have always known, that families can be together forever. I am ever thankful for the gospel in my life. I am thankful for my family and the honor and privilege I have been trusted with in raising *all* of my children. What a rich blessing! Families can be together forever.

5

SCOTT & MARCI'S STORY

We must learn to pray with meaning, "Not my will, but Thy will be done." When you are able to do this, his whisperings to you will be loud and clear.

—*Graham W. Doxey*[6]

I, like many women, assumed that I would grow up, get married, and have children. Little did I know that it wouldn't be an easy journey. To begin, I met and married my husband after serving a full-time mission to Raleigh, North Carolina. His little brother Cameron was an elder in the field, and we naturally became good friends. When I got home, I was offered a dinner invite from Cameron's family. (They happened to live in the same town where I would be attending school.) I politely said no, but Cameron's mother was persistent and wouldn't take no for an answer. I felt a little awkward, mainly because I was a freshly returned missionary, and, more important, because Cameron was still in the mission field. To add to my anxiety, I arrived and found the dinner to be a birthday celebration for their eldest son, Scott. There was a large crowd of family and friends who had gathered, and of course I faced the relentless question of who I was and what was I doing there. I was beginning to wonder myself!

I almost feigned illness, but I endured the night and was even able to laugh about it later in the privacy of my own car.

About a week later, I got a call from Scott, asking me out. I was surprised, but I thought, *Why not?* We had a whirlwind romance and were engaged only four weeks later! I kept praying and getting the same peaceful answer that "Yes, he is the one."

We decided to wait to have children since I had some schooling to finish up, and we wanted to get some debt paid off. We waited for about three and a half years, and then my "clock" started ticking. We decided to try having children. I assumed it would come easily. My family hadn't had prior problems conceiving. Six months passed. Then a year passed. I went to the doctor and was prescribed some ovulation medication. Another six months passed—still nothing. I went for another consultation, and this time surgery was the recommended route. I had one surgery after another. Then I discovered I had stage-four endometriosis, which meant more medications and more waiting, hoping, and disappointment. I questioned so many things: my doctors, my body, even my faith.

My husband and I talked about the possibility of growing our family through adoption. I wasn't opposed to it, but I really wanted to be a medical miracle and get pregnant. We agreed to take the adoption classes through LDS Family Services (LDSFS), and by then I should have recognized my answer, but I was too blinded by my own stubbornness. I would feel so happy and peaceful during the adoption classes and my heart would burn when I heard about adoption miracles, yet I was still clinging to my hopes of having my own biological child, even though I would leave the doctor in tears most of the time. I knew that something had to give; I couldn't ride the emotional roller coaster ride I had been on for much longer. So, I gave myself over to God and told him that I was letting go and and letting him take charge of things for a while.

The final straw was when we were at the University of Utah medical center to see a fertility specialist. I had decided that whatever the outcome was, I would be at peace and accept it. After several tests and procedures, we were told that my chances at conceiving were about 6 percent. Our only option would be in vitro fertilization (IVF), and it would most likely take five to six tries. The heaping price tag made my heart sink. I said a silent prayer and asked Heavenly Father if I should abandon this option and have our children come to us through adoption. I was overcome by such a sense of peace and love that I started to cry. The doctors assumed I was distraught by the price of IVF and offered some payment plan options. I just told them it wouldn't be necessary because we weren't going to do it. As I left the doctor's that day, I felt as if a weight had been lifted off me. I later told my husband, "I got the answer I needed."

We were excited as we finished up the home study and paperwork. I busied myself by sewing baby blankets and buying diapers. I had faith that God was going to get us our baby. After waiting again for a little over two years with LDSFS, we got an email contact from a birth mom in Texas. She had seen our profile on an LDS adoption-related website that we had posted on as a way of expanding our options. We corresponded with this sweet birth mom via email and telephone for about two months. Her due date was rapidly approaching, and I went to my boss and told her about our newly anticipated addition. They threw a wonderful baby shower at work, and everyone's excitement and support was wonderful. I decided to wait and buy plane tickets at the last minute because we were still debating on driving or flying. I also had a small uneasy feeling gnawing at me because we hadn't heard from the birth mom for several days. Our caseworker reassured us it was fine. She said this often happened and not to worry—our birth mom was probably busy, getting ready for the big day.

My last day of work was coming up, and I knew I only had about a week to get everything ready before we headed out to Texas. I quit my job on a Friday, and on Monday our worst fears were confirmed. The birth mom had changed her mind. I was completely devastated. I literally shut myself in my own little world. I was so sad; I felt as if a hole had been ripped out of my heart. I also had to deal with numerous phone calls of those calling to congratulate us on our bundle of joy, only to find out the disheartening news. I was a mess and couldn't look beyond my pity. The littlest thing would send me into tears. Thank heavens for my sweet husband, who lovingly stood by my side.

The Lord, however, was watching over us, and I learned that when he closes a door, he will open a window. My miracle came a few weeks later when I received a phone call from an old high school friend. She told me she had an adoption situation that I might be interested in. I told her, "No thanks, I've been through enough, and I just need time to sort all this through." She kept calling me, however (every other day) and said she couldn't get me out of her head. She said I just needed to see this little boy because she felt that he needed to be in our family. I finally relented, mainly because I wanted her to stop bugging me. However, there was a small part of me that was curious and a little hopeful.

This particular little boy had been in the foster care system for about four months. He had been removed from his home due to drug exposure. He was currently with another family, but they weren't looking to adopt. I was nervous for our first meeting. We just met at my friend's house, where she was tending him for the day. We instantly fell in love! He crawled right up to us and held out his arms. My heart melted. He was absolutely beautiful. His name was Dayce, and I just knew that this was our little boy.

We immediately checked into what we needed to do in order to take over as Dayce's foster parents. While we waited for everything to come together in the foster care system, my husband and I would see him at his foster home and play with him as often as we could. He was eleven months old at the time.

A short while later, he was in our home. We were hopeful that the next step would go quickly and that we would soon be able to adopt this little boy. However, nothing is easy, and we ran into a lot of conflict and anger with his birth mom, who was still trying to get parental custody. I was always civil and nice, regardless of how mean she was, but it was so hard to have Dayce ripped from my arms, crying, when his birth mom's visits came around weekly. Over time, though, his birth mom softened and was actually quite nice on occasion.

One day at a court hearing, she just sat and watched our family for several minutes. She finally came over to us, looking nervous. I wasn't sure what to expect. I clutched my little boy closer and cringed for what she might say. I was completely taken aback when she said that she saw how much we loved Dayce and how we could give him a two-parent home. She said she knew she would not be able to provide so many nice things for him. She asked if it would be possible for her to still see him if she were to relinquish her parental rights. I was flabbergasted! This was not what we were expecting at all.

The series of events that happened next were sudden. Within about two months, everything was finalized and in order. We realized how lucky we were to only be involved in the foster system for about one year.

Dayce had just celebrated his second birthday. Everything was wonderful, but I still wanted the infant experience. Don't get me wrong, we were able to see a lot of Dayce's firsts, but I longed for a baby also. I felt so selfish wanting this. I didn't dare say anything to my husband when I started to get promptings about another child coming. Then one day I got my courage up and asked how he felt about getting another child before the end of the year. He laughed and said I was baby hungry because I had so many pregnant friends. This was the end of July 2004. I thought, *Am I crazy?* Heavenly Father had already blessed me so much, especially by taking away my strong desire for a biological child. I was having so much joy being a mother too; Dayce was at a delightful age. Why couldn't I just be content? Still the feelings kept coming. One day while Dayce was napping, I pulled out all my infant stuff from my baby shower. My husband came home from work early that day and discovered what I was doing. I again relayed my feelings about preparing for another child. He looked at me, smirked, and said, "I have had that feeling too, but I didn't want to admit you were right."

The next few weeks were full of questions. We were not currently with an agency and hadn't told anyone we were looking to adopt so quickly. I again put my trust in Heavenly Father and figured it would all work out. Well, I got a phone call from an old friend we had met through the adoption circle at an FSA conference. (FSA stands for Families Supporting Adoption, a group sponsored by LDSFS.) My friend said she had been thinking of us as a referral for an agency she was dealing with in Oklahoma called Adoption Choices. They had an African-American baby who would be needing a home, but they didn't have any families on their waiting list who would adopt a full African-American child. She asked, "Would you be interested?" Immediately, I knew this was our baby.

We started contacting the agency, but they were reluctant to work with us since we were out of state. They wanted us to fly out, do the paperwork there, and meet with their social workers. I didn't want to spend money on something so risky, so I pleaded with them to let us do everything via phone and fax. They finally relented, mostly, I think, because we were their only option. They certainly didn't make things easy for us, though. They required all kinds of medical tests and background checks that they insisted they needed right away. Again, we were being watched over by the Lord. Oftentimes, we would go to places and they would just be closing, but we happened to make it in the nick of time. One of the required tests was an HIV blood test that cost us $600 a piece to complete. We weren't sure we could afford this, but the money seemed to come from nowhere. We were very blessed. Another huge leap of faith was when we had to wire a substantial amount of money to the agency prior to our son's birth. As I dropped the cashier's check in the Fed Ex box, I was sweating bullets and just praying that the money would not be in vain.

It was about 4:30 on the morning of October 1 when we received the call that our birth mom's water had broken. They wanted us in Oklahoma as quickly as possible. This was a surprise, and my husband and I didn't think we would be able to make it until the following day with all the arrangements that were required. We had to get a hotel, purchase plane tickets, and arrange for a car rental. We also had to make arrangements for Dayce.

Again, miracles happened. I was on the computer and phone most of the morning, and by noon, we had our plane tickets, hotel, and car rental. Everything fell into place, and by 10:20 that night, we arrived in Oklahoma City. We rushed to the hospital to see our perfect little angel. We decided to name him Trey. I wanted so badly to meet the birth mom, but she requested that the adoption be closed. Sadly, we have little information on my son's birth family, not even a picture.

We spent a week in Oklahoma, hoping that our ICPC (Interstate Compact on the Placement of Children) would clear soon. The Oklahoma agency told us that typically it took ten to fourteen days. In my excitement to see my son, I hadn't been thinking clearly when I had bought our plane tickets, and we were scheduled to come home exactly one week after his birth. This was nowhere near the ten- to fourteen-day waiting period. The day that we were supposed to go home, my husband was about to go down to the lobby and make arrangements for us to stay a few more days when we got a phone call from the agency. They told us that our ICPC had been cleared about ten minutes previously, and we were free to take our son home. She informed us that this had never happened so quickly with any other adoption case they had. I knew that it was the Lord again watching out for our little family. We had little time to spare as we raced to get to the airport and catch our plane.

Life was good; we were enjoying our little family and thought that perhaps two children was plenty. The years passed; Dayce was five, and Trey had recently turned three. Once again, though, I started getting "the feeling." I turned to Heart to Heart, having heard positive things from other friends who had adopted there. I submitted our paperwork in May of 2006.

Soon after this I received another phone call to foster a little four-year-old girl. She was African-American, and her current foster family knew little of how to care for her hair and skin. I wondered if maybe this was our opportunity. She came to our home and was a delight. However, it was challenging and tiring having our children so close in age.

In the meantime, I received several calls about possible adoption situations, but for whatever reason, they never seemed to work out. I was getting kind of discouraged. It was looking very likely that our foster daughter would return to her parents soon, so that wasn't going to work out for us. The end of the year was fast approaching, and I felt like I was sinking with all of my responsibilities. My husband and I decided that if we didn't hear anything by the end of the year, we would forgo our ventures to adopt any more children. It was about two weeks before Christmas when we received a phone call from the agency, asking us to do a conference call with a birth mom. We had done this before and nothing had worked out, but I agreed anyway.

The evening came, and we got to talk to a sweet yet shy birth mom. I have this nervous talking thing, so I assumed I had scared her off because I just couldn't shut up! Much to our surprise, the agency called back the following night and said the birth mom wanted to go to dinner with our family and that we should bring along the kids. I was nervous, to say the least. You see, our kids were not exactly the quiet, sit-still type. They were typical rambunctious boys. Our idea of eating out was the drive-up window. We braced ourselves for the worst. When we arrived at Olive Garden, we pleaded with our boys to be on their best behavior. Much to our astonishment, they behaved like perfect gentle-men, adding charm and wit at all the right times. Everyone kept commenting on how surprised they were that our children behaved so well for their ages. I have to admit I was completely surprised too.

The birth mom disclosed that she was currently parenting a four-year-old son and was unable to provide for her unborn child. She had originally picked a family with no other children, but the adoptive parents had changed their minds at the last minute. She said maybe it would be a good thing for her little girl to have some brothers. We were shocked. We were going to be a mom and dad to a little baby girl!

The next few days were a blur. I went shopping with the birth mom and got to spend quite a bit of one-on-one time with her. Her sister flew out from Delaware, and we got to meet her as well. It was a wonderful experience that we will always cherish. We hadn't told our families a thing, so we completely stunned them with the news at our Christmas party. In the past, we always had Santa Claus come and deliver the children new pajamas for their gift. This time I had written a note saying that Scott and Marci were getting a baby girl. I tucked the note inside an envelope, and when Santa read it, the looks on our family members' faces were priceless. They were so excited for us!

That night after the children were asleep, and I was still awake, wrapping gifts, the phone rang at about 9:30. It was our caseworker telling us our birth mom was on her way to the hospital. I rushed to get down there in time but was too late to be in the delivery room. Our daughter, Kalli, was born December 21, 2006, weighing in at a whopping 10 lbs. and 11 oz. Our little petite birth mom was such a trooper! Because Kalli had jaundice, they didn't allow us to bring her home until a few days later. It happened to be on Christmas Day, in fact! It was definitely the best gift ever. We invited the birth mom and her sister back to our home to spend the Christmas holiday with us. It was so nice, and we hold many dear memories from that visit.

Our little foster girl stayed with us for another couple of months after that. Although she stayed with us for about eight months in all, she ultimately went back to her birth family. Having her with us was a growing experience for all of us, and we feel it helped our family for the better, though it was definitely bittersweet to say the least.

We are so blessed to be part of adoption. Our children are keeping us young and busy. My oldest, Dayce, is now eight. Trey is six, and Kalli just turned three. I feel so incredibly lucky to be a mother to such wonderful spirits of our Heavenly Father. Much to my husband's relief, I feel whole with our three little children, and I haven't gotten any more "feelings." I know that we are blessed to be part of the adoption journey, and I thank Heavenly Father every day for our experiences.

6

DAVID & KRISTIN'S STORY

Progress is accelerated when you willingly allow Him to lead you through every growth experience you encounter. . . . When you trust in the Lord, when you are willing to let your heart and your mind be centered in His will, when you ask to be led by the Spirit to do His will, you are assured of the greatest happiness along the way.

—*Richard G. Scott*[7]

When David and I got married, I was thirty-four and he was twenty-one. We knew that because of my age, we wouldn't have a lot of time to have children. We figured we'd have a couple and adopt a couple. We were really excited when two weeks after getting married, I discovered I was pregnant, but then we were devastated eight weeks later when I miscarried. After two more years of trying, including infertility pills, artificial insemination, and shots, we were ready to adopt.

We tried to adopt for three and a half years with LDS Family Services but didn't have any luck. Finally we found an attorney who specialized in adoptions, and he recommended an agency for us. At that point, we were emotionally exhausted and losing hope.

After about three months, we got a call about a little boy that would be born in Nebraska. I had always thought I would have a boy first, and we were happy to hear that the little boy would be white. It seemed like that would be easier for us and for him. We then learned that some of our paperwork hadn't been handled correctly, and that if the baby was born in the next couple of days, our paperwork wouldn't be ready and we wouldn't be able to adopt him. We packed our bags and a bag for the little one and just hoped for the best. We prayed about it but weren't sure if it was the right thing. I finally prayed and told Heavenly Father that I couldn't make the decision. It was just too emotional. I told him that I was going to take this baby unless he took it away from me. If the little boy wasn't meant to be ours, Heavenly Father would have to stop it from happening. The birth mom went into labor that night, so we were unable to adopt. Once again we were emotionally devastated, and I was ready to give up.

Just about a week later, we learned about another birth mom. We didn't know if she was having a girl or a boy, but from the time we learned about her, we knew that this little baby was meant to be a part of our family. My heart was calm, and I didn't worry like I had in the past. I was still nervous, but I was filled with a sense of peace. We knew that both the parents were black, and we had concerns because we had friends and family members that were African-American who had told us that a black child raised by white parents would most likely be rejected by the black community. We decided that we would just love this baby and do the best that we could. We'd address any issues as they came to us, but in the meantime, we would just do the best we could and trust that God would send us the baby that was right for us.

Two days before the baby was born, I got a call from my best friend from high school. She had a family member that was getting ready to deliver twins, a girl and a boy, and she wondered if we were interested in adopting them. It was amazing because previously this would have seemed like the perfect situation—an agency-free adoption that would be less expensive, a girl and a boy, white, from a family that we knew. But I knew that our baby was waiting to be born and that it was going to be a little black baby.

As I mentioned earlier, I had always thought we'd have a boy first. But just before the baby was born, I knew she was going to be a girl. I told my mom that we needed to hurry and go buy some little girl clothes. We were in line at Kohl's buying pink clothes when I got a text message telling me that the baby had been born—it was a girl. I started sobbing in the line at Kohl's and probably scared all the other shoppers.

Our adoption was closed, so we had to wait two days before we could go get Baylie. It was the longest two days of my life. I thought of her birth mom, lying there in the hospital. I thought of Baylie all alone in the nursery and hoped someone was holding her. Finally, we got to go pick her up. It seemed unreal at first, and I kept waiting for someone to come take her back. But it didn't take long before I knew that we would all be together forever. Heavenly Father sent us the sweetest, most beautiful little girl. I can't imagine having any other baby.

I'm not sure why it was so hard for us to get Baylie. We'd been married almost six years before we finally got her. I turned forty only five weeks after we got her. It's been a long time coming, but she was well worth the wait.

7

KEN & KATHRYN'S STORY

Remember, in the world before we came here, faithful women were given certain assignments while faithful men were foreordained to certain priesthood tasks. While we do not now remember the particulars, this does not alter the glorious reality of what we once agreed to.

—*Spencer W. Kimball*[8]

Our adoption story started out seven years ago. We were just starting to look into adoption, researching agencies and figuring out how we were going to pay for it. I was at work on August 13 and was out doing home visits. At the time, I was working for Child Protective Services. I remember my cell ringing, and a friend of mine who also works in the field asked me where we were in the adoption process. I told her that we were looking into it but that we had none of the paperwork completed. She asked me how soon we would consider it. I told her as soon as it was right, not knowing exactly what she was getting at. Then she told me that a baby boy had been born the night before and that if we wanted him, he was ours. I was completely silent as the tears formed. Somehow I pulled myself together enough to ask her what she meant. She explained that she had come across a girl who wanted to place her new baby for adoption. The girl wasn't working with an agency or with an attorney, and she didn't want to pick the family; she just wanted a good two-parent home for her son. My friend had immediately thought of us. All I could think of was to say, "I have to call Ken." Then I hung up.

Ken was up in Park City with a number of his guy friends. The only way I knew to reach him was on his best friend's cell phone. So I called and asked Dave for Ken. Ken got on the phone, and I asked him to leave the group, which he did. I told him what had happened, and his only response was, "I'm on my way home."

We never discussed if we would take the baby. It was like we just knew this baby was ours. We never said, "So what do you think?" It was just understood. Ken got home, and I had called my friend back. We agreed to go and see the baby in the hospital. Initially, Sophia, the baby's birth mother, did not want to meet us, but she authorized us to come and see the baby in the hospital. Ken and I went up there and were spending time with him when my friend came in and said that Sophia had changed her mind and wanted to meet us. We were totally dumbfounded. What do you say to someone who is giving you her child? Uh, gee, thanks? But we knew we didn't want to pass this opportunity up, so we agreed.

We had no idea what to expect, and I am sure she didn't either. But we went in her room, with my friend, and spent about two hours with her. Somehow we found things to talk about. We learned more about her; she was from the Ogden area and had been with the birth father in an ongoing relationship for awhile, but when he found out she was pregnant, he bolted. She hadn't seen him since. She herself was raised without a father. Her father was just now trying to get back into her life, and she was having a hard time with it. She told us she wanted *more* for her baby. She wanted him to have a father in his life.

She asked us about us: where we were from, why we couldn't have kids, what we wanted to name him, what our families were going to think of this. And, odd as it was, she kept thanking us. It seemed so strange—she was the one giving us the most amazing gift in the world, and she was thanking us. She thanked us for giving him everything she wouldn't be able to. We thanked her for giving us something we never thought we would have. Sophia was amazing. She was a very small girl, especially for just giving birth twenty-four hours before, and she had long dark hair pulled into a bun and huge brown eyes. She was beautiful, and our son is the spitting image of her. I will never forget the way Ken just sobbed after meeting her. He was so overwhelmed by the emotion and by what she was doing for us. I so wished we could have adopted her too. We talked about what kind of contact to have afterward, and she said that she wanted letters and pictures on occasion through the attorney handling the adoption. We agreed to that. We sent a few things over during the next few months and then never heard from her.

We called our families and told them. They really didn't know what to say, but they were excited. We took the following day off work and burned plastic like you wouldn't believe. We had less than twenty-four hours to bring home a baby! We had so much fun at Target and Wal-Mart, picking up necessities. I was amazed that just by making one call to my friend Laneece, the word quickly spread and we had more than we could have ever needed to bring him home. People opened their hearts and wallets and were so generous.

We brought Joshua home five years ago. Our family left after Joshua was asleep, but he woke up a few hours later, as newborns do. I made him a bottle, wondering if it was warm enough, if there was enough formula for him, if I would know when to burp him. The whole time I was just sitting there in total disbelief that he was ours. We were parents.

We didn't realize it at the time, but now, knowing how typical adoptions work, we can see that the Lord's hand was in everything that happened. For one thing, Ken and I didn't have a home study done, no background checks completed, nothing. Yet a judge awarded us custody of Joshua without those things, pending the adoption being finalized six months later. This never happens. Judges almost always require some kind of screening before giving people children, but this judge was moved to do so anyway.

The second miracle that took place had to do with finances. Adoption is extremely expensive—think second mortgage expensive. Ken was teaching and making $28,000 a year at that point, and I was making about eleven dollars an hour for the state. We had two car loans, a new mortgage, and no money for this kind of thing. But it all worked out. My friend, an attorney I knew from work, would only let me pay her for the filing fees to the court ($130) for her part in this. Then we paid for a home study a few months later. It was like the widow's mite. We gave what we had and were still blessed with the child Heavenly Father wanted for us. The Lord had heard our prayers. He knew our circumstances and paved a way for us.

The last miracle was the time. We didn't have to wait. We weren't on the books with an agency. Happily for us, Joshua practically fell into our laps. He is our miracle baby. We tell him often of his birth mother, his adoption, and how lucky we are to have him.

Our story continues at the beginning of July 2005. I was thinking the spacing between the children would be perfect, since Joshua was almost two at that point. Ken was hesitant only because of the money issue (just a minor detail). He was, after all, in grad school, working two jobs, and very busy. I kept pushing, though, feeling like we needed to move forward. One day we were in church, listening to our stake patriarch speak on free agency, prayer, and finding the right answers for us. He said that sometimes we feel we have to pray over everything we do. He said that if any of us were deliberating over a major decision, we should move forward with it, and if it wasn't right, we would know that it wasn't, and then we would have our answer. So I took that as our answer. We were to move forward. Ken agreed.

We got our home study updated. Then we went on vacation. We went to Missouri, to the Lake of the Ozarks. During that whole trip I couldn't help but think that there was someone coming soon to our family. I told Ken I couldn't wait to get back and jump right into this adoption thing again.

We got back, and Ken started school again, both grad school and his teaching job. I updated our profile, and we contacted TLC Adoptions and sent them all of our paperwork. Within a day we were called to say that our profile was being shown to a birth mom in Alabama. Unfortunately, she ended up not choosing us. Then Sandy, a caseworker for TLC adoptions, called us about a situation in Georgia. She said that there was a fourteen-month-old little girl named Janae, who her mother was placing. She asked if we were open to it. We told her to show our profile to this mom. The birth mother chose our family but then later decided to keep her baby. I couldn't help but think that there was something more out there for us, even though this hadn't worked out. Also we loved the name Janae, so we decided that when the time came and we did adopt a little girl, her name would be Janae.

After that I got an email from Sandy. She said that she had just gotten word about a preemie born in Texas. The baby girl was extremely fragile medically. She had been born at twenty-six weeks. She was on a ventilator, feeding tube, and a bunch of other scary medical things. She asked if we were open to this situation. I asked, "Where in Texas is the baby from?" Texas is, after all, a huge state. Sandy double checked the records. She had been born in Houston, at St. Joseph's hospital, right downtown, twenty-five minutes from the place where I grew up and where my parents were still living. I was hesitant because of the medical issues but felt good about it. Ken and I felt we needed priest-hood blessings. We asked our home teachers to give them to us. We were told very clearly that we were to take her. We were also told that she was meant for our family and that by adopting her, it would be the only way she would have the gospel in this life. How do you say no to an answer that direct? You don't.

We called Sandy and said we were on board 100 percent. I don't think she really believed us. She tried to scare us (and she did) with facts about preemies, brain bleeds, ventilators, and so forth, but we told her to still present us to the agency in Houston. They showed the birth mother our profile, and we were chosen on Wednesday, September 28, 2005. We flew to Houston the next evening and met Janae Friday morning. There was something completely surreal about that moment. I should have been scared. I normally would have been intimidated by all of the NICU equipment around her and the other sick babies, but I wasn't scared. We were just glad they let us hold her. We both cried.

She was so extremely little. She had been 1.8 lbs. at birth. Now, at that point, she was a beefy 3.5. She was bundled up so much, with a pink crocheted hat on. When I held her the first time, she opened her eyes, and she stayed awake for most of that first day we spent with her. This was significant for many reasons. For one thing, she had only rarely opened her eyes prior to that day. Gestationally she was only thirty-four weeks along at that point, and at that stage babies don't typically open their eyes much. But I think she knew she was meeting her family!

That day was so fun but overwhelming. They let us bathe her, change her diaper, and dress her; it was so special. They showed us how to change her oxygen tube, how to feed her, how to give her the meds, and how to work the monitors that would come home with us. We met around a big conference table with her "team" of about a dozen people who had all been working with her. There was a neonatologist, a cardiologist, a neurologist, an occupational therapist, a physical therapist, a respiratory therapist, a pulmonologist, the head nurse, the main nurse, a social worker, and the agency director. I am sure they were "feeling us out," but we were just focused on Janae.

She stayed in the hospital a few more days, and then she was released to us. We took her back to my parents' house and waited for the clearance to come back to Utah with her. The first night home, Janae stopped eating. For a regular newborn, you wouldn't sweat this too much, but Janae had to eat 40 CCs every three hours to maintain her weight. She didn't eat all night. We rushed her back to the NICU, and they readmitted her for another seventy-two hours. As it turned out, she had just gotten cold, but at that stage, her whole body had sort of gone into shock, and she stopped eating. As soon as they put her on the warming bed, she was fine. Her head nurse, Sherry, joked that Janae had just missed her NICU family and wanted to come back and see them.

Well, that was it. Janae's birth mom, Yolanda, had placed her up for adoption right at birth. Yolanda was overwhelmed by the unknowns of having such a medically fragile child when she was already a struggling single mother to three other girls. Yolanda never met us. But we were told by her social worker that she just knew she couldn't do it. She couldn't adequately take care of Janae with everything else on her plate. I respect Yolanda and love her tremendously for giving us this opportunity. We do know some things about her, like her favorite color, movie, music, sports teams, and a few things about her own family. That kind of information will be good to share with Janae as she gets older.

It's hard to believe it has already been five years. In many ways, the first year was a blur—all of the weekly doctor appointments, medical equipment, and bills. But we were told to move forward, we did, and we were blessed every step of the way.

We feel that we experienced many tender mercies along our road to transracial adoption. Several of them were financial. We took out a second mortgage to pay for Janae's adoption. We weren't sure where the money would come from to pay the additional mortgage, but while we were in Houston with her, we checked our account balance. Ken had received an unexpected raise. The monthly difference in what he was now making was exactly what we needed to pay the second mortgage, to the penny: $204.16.

Another blessing was that Janae was born in Houston. With our extremely limited budget, we could afford the airfare, but not the accommodations of traveling to get a baby. What a miracle that in all the places she could be born, she was right by my parents! We stayed in their home, ate their food, and drove their cars for those three weeks.

And even though Janae's medical bills were pretty hefty that first year, we had incredible insurance to pay most of it, and somehow we were able to pay the rest. Not a small feat for a baby like Janae, but it all worked out.

We love our girl. She is a walking miracle and such a blessing. I have to remind myself these days that she was ever that fragile, as she has no lasting effects of prematurity. We love our daughter Janae! We can't imagine our life without her.

8

IVAN & MELISSA'S STORY

Too frequently, women underestimate their influence for good. Well could you follow the formula given by the Lord: "Establish a house, even a house of prayer, a house of fasting, a house of faith, a house of learning, a house of glory, a house of order, a house of God" (D&C 88:119). In such a house will be found happy, smiling children who have been taught, by precept and example, the truth. In a Latter-day Saint home, children are not simply tolerated, but welcomed; not commanded, but encouraged; not driven, but guided; not neglected, but loved.

—Thomas S. Monson[9]

Ivan and I were married in the Jordan River Temple on December 14, 2002. We were both excited to start a family. We talked about having children of our own, and then, later, adopting two black children. I have two cousins who are biracial and adopted, so I thought that would be wonderful. Ivan always seemed to know that we would adopt. I got pregnant six months after we got married, and we welcomed our beautiful daughter, Savannah, in April 2004. When she was ten months old, we started trying for baby number two. Two years passed, and we had no luck getting pregnant. We tried one round of

Clomid, but infertility treatments just didn't seem right for us. The Spirit spoke to both of us, and we just knew it was time to adopt. Although many friends and family members questioned our decision, we knew this was the path the Lord wanted us to take. A week after we had submitted our profile to our adoption agency, we received a phone call. The agency had a particular birth mother in mind for us. From the moment the agency told us her name, I felt calm and at peace. I knew that this was our birth mother. I knew she would choose us and that this would be our baby. I wasn't nervous at all, and a week later the agency called to tell us what I already knew: that the birth mother had chosen us. Before this situation, we had been involved in an adoption where the birth mom had ultimately decided to keep her baby. During the first situation, each day was full of drama and anxiety. With this situation, there were peaceful feelings, and I knew it was all going to work out just fine.

Rhonda, the birth mom, was supposed to be induced on a Monday. The Thursday before, we met with her to have dinner. The conversation was fun and lively. We, along with some of the girls from the agency, decided to guess the time of birth for the baby. She was set to be induced at 7:00 AM, and I guessed 10:30 AM. Everyone groaned and told me that it would never go that fast, but I stuck by my prediction. That weekend, I told my husband, "I think that Rhonda's water is going to break. I don't think she is going to have to be induced." The weekend passed, and no phone calls came about Rhonda's water breaking, but in my heart, I just knew she wasn't going to be induced. Sunday night, we prepared to go to the hospital in the morning and said our prayers. At midnight we were woken by a phone call—Rhonda's water had broken.

We went to the hospital at about 6:00 AM and waited. Our little Sienna was born at 10:31 AM. She was the most beautiful baby. The moments we had in the hospital with her and with Rhonda were amazing. We feel so lucky to have this adorable little girl in our lives. Adoption is the most beautiful thing. You feel the hand of the Lord in your life like you never have before. Everything has to come together so perfectly, and you know that the Lord is guiding it or it would never happen. We were sealed to our little princess six months later, and the following month I found out I was pregnant. So now we have our three sweet princesses, and we thank the Lord every day for putting our family together in such a beautiful way.

9

GREG & STEPHANIE'S STORY

Now, I testify [the Spirit] is a small voice. It whispers, not shouts. And so you must be very quiet inside. That is why you may wisely fast when you want to listen. And that is why you will listen best when you feel, "Father, thy will, not mine, be done." You will have a feeling of "I want what you want." Then, the still small voice will seem as if it pierces you. It may make your bones to quake. More often it will make your heart burn within . . . which will lift and reassure.

—Henry B. Eyring[10]

Greg and I started our adoption journey the summer of 2005. We had talked about adopting a baby girl for a few years but just talked about it. We were not really sure if we would ever act on it until one Sunday. We were sitting in sacrament meeting, and while the sacrament was being passed, my mind wandered between things. All of a sudden, I had this overwhelming thought about adoption. Something told me that we were going to adopt a baby girl. I turned to Greg and said, "We better start the adoption process because we're supposed to have a baby girl."

A week later, we started our home study. With our home study done, I started searching the Internet for different agencies. I was so consumed with the whole idea that I spent hours on the Internet, reading different articles and looking for agencies. I next turned to the yellow pages and started calling all the Utah agencies. This was around November 2005. Yes, it was four months later, and we still didn't have our papers in anywhere. I called five agencies and got information sent to me, talked with a few people that I had heard of through other friends that had adopted, talked to several other people about their agencies, and still could not make up my mind. During this time, my sister ran into a friend of hers that she had not seen in years. Her friend had just adopted their second baby from an agency here in Salt Lake City called Children's Service Society. I had not called that agency, so I decided to contact them. I called and spoke to someone early in December. I requested a packet and left it at that. With the holidays around the corner, I put the adoption on hold.

One night I had a dream about a beautiful little African-American girl. The next morning, I told Greg that our baby girl was going to be African-American, not Caucasian. He just looked at me and said, "Okay." In January I set my New Year's resolution to pick an agency and be done with the searching. After months of praying and pondering, we decided on an agency. At the end of January, on a Tuesday, we sent in our paperwork, along with our profile to A Guardian Angel Adoptions. On Friday of that same week, I was at work when I got a call from Children's Service Society. The conversation started out like this: "Hi, this is Katie from CSS. You had contacted us in December, inquiring about adopting a baby girl. We had an African-American baby girl born this morning in Kentucky that is in need of a home, and your name came to my mind. I have contacted three other families, and they all need time to think about it, but we are in a rush because her birth mom wants to leave the hospital in the morning, and we need to place her today." My heart literally sank, and I felt like I was going to pass out because of the overwhelming feeling that came over me. I started crying and said, "Yes, we will take her."

I didn't know any of the details about this baby, nor had I okayed it with Greg, but I told her I would be on a plane as soon as I could. I hung up the phone and everyone in my office was looking at me like someone had just died. My boss had to call Greg and tell him the news because I was so emotional that I could barely talk. I soon realized that we were taking a huge leap of faith with this situation because I didn't know any details about her birth mother—if she used drugs or alcohol. I didn't even know if the baby was healthy . . . nothing. I just knew that it felt right, and I was totally leaving it in the hands of our Father in Heaven. The plane ride to Kentucky was dreadful. Katie from CSS was nice enough to offer to go with me to make the transition easy for the birth mom, since I was a complete stranger, walking into her hospital room and taking her new baby girl from her. I just kept thinking in my mind that there was no way this girl was going to give a complete stranger her baby.

To make a long story short, all went well. The birth mother relinquished her rights, and we were able to sign a few days later. When I asked Kenley's birth mother how she came into contact with an agency from Utah, she said, "I don't know, something just felt like I wanted this baby to have a family from Utah because I had heard good things about families in Utah." She had no idea what was telling her, but I knew.

I'm so very thankful to my Father in Heaven for directing this baby girl into our family. There is no doubt in my mind that this little girl was meant to be in our family. She has been such a blessing in our home, and we love her so much. These last few years have gone by so fast, and I can't believe Kenley is already four. I wouldn't trade the experience for anything.

10

ALICIA & MIKE'S STORY

Some time ago, Nate, then just over three, said: "Mommy, there is another little girl who is supposed to come to our family. She has dark hair and dark eyes and lives a long way from here." The wise mother asked, "How do you know this?" "Jesus told me, upstairs." The mother noted, "We don't have an upstairs," but quickly sensed the significance of what had been communicated. After much travail and many prayers, the Barker family were in a sealing room in the Salt Lake Temple in the fall of 1995—where a little girl with dark hair and dark eyes, from Kazakhstan, was sealed to them for time and eternity. Inspired children still tell parents "great and marvelous things" (3 Nephi 26:14).

—Neal A. Maxwell[11]

I guess to understand how Morgan came to our family you'll need to know a little bit about what happened before she arrived. Alex is our biological son and he is nine years older than Morgan. It took a couple of years for him to arrive, though. I was actually at the fertility doctor's office, walking out with a prescription for Clomid when the nurse ran out to get us and said we just had to come back in and look at my pregnancy test. It was pretty amazing—two pink lines. Yes! Finally, I was pregnant.

Later, I had a doctor tell us that Alex was a miracle child and that chances were we wouldn't be able to conceive again. What did he know? We had done it once, why not again? I think that's where my heart got in trouble. I really believed we would fill out our paperwork and I would get pregnant again, or that we would adopt and I would get pregnant again. I never expected to adopt because there was no other choice.

We filled out paperwork before we did infertility testing. Mike is in the computer industry, and in 2001–2003 we were employed, laid off, employed, laid off. Often we didn't have company health insurance, so I was afraid to be tested for fear I wouldn't be able to get health insurance. In 2003 we went ahead and filled out the paperwork, and in 2004 we were approved. We were in Florida at the time, and Mike was going to graduate school there. We thought for sure we could easily adopt a black child there since most adoptive parents there are white and against transracial families with white parents and black children. Our social worker even said, "You would take a *black* child?" I had pretty high hopes after that comment!

In February of 2005, we were back in Alpine, and a little three-year-old black boy, Michael, came up for adoption through a lawyer friend of ours. I thought it would have to be right. Michael had lost his mother, he had no father, and his guardian was a lawyer in the same office where our friend worked. I was even able to talk to Michael on the phone and hear his sweet voice.

Unfortunately, we were unemployed since Mike had just finished school. He had initially taken a job, but when we came back to Utah, they changed the job description to selling, and if you know my husband, he's a computer geek, so selling just didn't work. He was struggling *again* to find employment. But we knew the money would work itself out. Michael needed a family and a mom; we needed a child and a son. We had the gospel to help him, and we knew he'd be so much better off with us. I thought it was meant to be. But something didn't feel right.

Michael had some problems, but nothing I didn't think we, the Lord, and the gospel couldn't help. However, the situation was serious enough that we talked with our bishop. While talking he read to us Alma 29. As he was reading he said, "This is a missionary chapter.

I'm not sure why I'm reading this." Later that night I went up to my mother's house and sobbed on her lap, telling her that I couldn't understand why I was getting a "No" answer and why I had to be the one to say "No." I remember saying to her, "If it was right, I wouldn't be sitting here with you, I'd be on a plane. But I'm not on that plane! Something is wrong."

The next morning we told the lawyers no. After Mike went to work and Alex went to school, I was left to grieve by myself again. I pulled out my scriptures and reread Alma 29. There were a few verses that stood out to me, and I felt the spirit.

> O that I were an angel, and could have the wish of mine heart.
>
> I am a man, and do sin in my wish; for I ought to be content with the things which the Lord hath allotted unto me.
>
> For I know that he granteth unto men according to the desire whether it be unto death or unto life; yea, I know that he allotteth unto men, yea, decreeth unto them decrees which are unalterable, according to their wills, whether they be unto salvation or unto destruction. Yea, and I know that good and evil have come before all men; he that knoweth not good from evil is blameless. (v. 1, 3–5)

For me these verses opened my understanding, and I had my answer as to why little Michael wasn't going to come to us. I'm not sure he would have been able to live up to what he would have known was right within the parameters of the gospel, and with the knowledge we would have given him, he would have been held accountable. I also felt that he needed to stay within his race and that adding the burden of being black in a mostly white area might just be too much for him with the other trials he was going to face.

I am not a Molly Mormon or a scriptural person by any means. My answers don't usually come through the scriptures. I don't believe that most people would have interpreted these verses as I did, but I do know how the Spirit read it to me on that day, and the peace the Lord gave me in the strong sadness and grief I felt. The grief carried on for a few more months, but deep down I knew we were right in our decision, as sad as it was, and I didn't have to revisit the choice.

In the late summer of 2005, we were living in Alpine, Mike was employed, and things were better financially, so we thought maybe we should try in vitro. We met with a doctor in American Fork, and after running tests, he said there was no way we would conceive without medical intervention. He also said that because of our unique situation, the local doctors would not be able to help us. He referred us to a place in California that would harvest twenty of my eggs and then insert the sperm into the egg. They would insert four fertilized eggs into me and hope that one, but not all, would take. What would I do if I had twins or even more multiples? I didn't feel that I could handle it. On top of that, I would come home with sixteen eggs that would be in storage at $250 a year.

That week my mom taped a *60 Minutes* program about women who had this done and then placed for adoption their extra fertilized eggs. This put me in a huge conflict. I was asking to adopt a child, but I wasn't ready to place my own eggs for adoption. But how could I destroy those eggs when there were couples just like me, wanting more children? On the other hand, how could I place my future children for adoption? I felt very selfish. I think my desire for children made placing my eggs for adoption a situation my brain couldn't handle, and it just didn't feel right to go to California and proceed on that path. So that put us back on the adoption path again. This time it was our only option.

All these experiences made me sad, sometimes bitter, and they made me question my testimony and my relationship with God. My patriarchal blessing says, "You will be privileged to be co-creators with your Father in Heaven in creating bodies that little spirits might have a tabernacle in which to dwell as they come to this earth." I think this is why I was so sure I would conceive again. I felt like it was a cruel joke for God to put something like that in my blessing when he knew I would struggle with this problem and knew that I would come to my blessing for answers. I had a testimony of my blessing as I had watched the course of my life follow my blessing. But around this time I went through a great period of questioning if the patriarch was really ordained by God; for if he said things that were incorrect, then the priesthood wasn't true, which made the gospel not true. It wasn't a very pretty time for me since I was so very angry at God and very depressed.

After losing little Michael and then Ethan, another baby we held, I was praying and pondering, and I realized that I was on this path because I needed to become what the Lord needed me to become so that I could live with him again. I finally submitted to him. The refiner's fire is indeed difficult, but the beauty that is achieved in the end is worth it. Wouldn't we all do whatever we could to live with our Heavenly Father again? I can tell you I wasn't the least bit happy to receive this answer, but I promised him I would do it. (This was still about three months before I got the answer that we really did need to adopt.)

We believe one of the reasons Heavenly Father gave us this experience was to help us understand what it was like having to make the right decision when your heart wants to make another—just like a birth mom does.

During this time I did some research on transracial adoptions. I wanted to make sure we knew what we were getting ourselves and our future baby into. Nothing I read made me feel like our decision was wrong or made me afraid of what the future would bring. We were calm and knew the Lord would help us through anything. We knew that there would be sacrifices along the way, but we felt ready for a transracial family. I always knew we were looking for our baby, the one that was supposed to be in our family. We weren't just looking for a child for our home, we were looking for *the* child that God was sending to our home.

In January of 2007 we had another situation come our way. We went to visit the birth mother in the hospital. Because of the pain I had been feeling, I hadn't held or even looked at a baby for about six years—it was just too hard for me. The birth mother decided to bring in the baby and then placed him in my arms and let me feed him. I cried and felt so attached to him. About fourteen days later, the birth mother decided to parent herself.

We were so sad that we decided we were finished with the adoption process. We couldn't handle that kind of pain again. It just couldn't be worth it. We decided three family members were okay, even if it didn't feel like our full family—we were a family nonetheless.

I had listened to a conference talk by Elder Richard G. Scott in April 2007 that seemed to validate my feelings. He said,

> What do you do when you have prepared carefully, have prayed fervently, waited a reasonable time for a response, and still do not feel an answer? You may want to express thanks when that occurs, for it is an evidence of his trust. When you are living worthily and your choice

is consistent with the Savior's teachings and you need to act, proceed with trust. As you are sensitive to the promptings of the Spirit, one of two things will certainly occur at the appropriate time: either the stupor of thought will come, indicating an improper choice, or the peace or the burning in the bosom will be felt, confirming that your choice was correct. When you are living righteously and are acting with trust, God will not let you proceed too far without a warning impression if you have made the wrong decision.[12]

I continued down the path of no adopting. Then about a month later on May 3, Heavenly Father gave me that warning impression. My mother was talking to me on the phone and said, "I hope that you can rest this summer. You've been so busy with all the things you are doing . . . I hope that you'll take some time to slow down and rest."

My answer to her was a telling one, and it came without thought: "If I stop running, I'll have to feel, and I wouldn't want to do that." Suddenly I realized we had a problem. I was running, and the Lord was telling me we were making an improper choice, just as Elder Scott had said he would.

I cried to my friend that night and told her I just didn't know how to open myself up to do it again, but the second answer came—if the Lord thought we could, then we would. I called another adoptive mom and told her I was ready to move forward. She gave me some more adoption names and phone numbers, and we were on our way again.

At one point during our four-year adoption process, a lady said to me, "You will know it's time and your baby is ready when you can't think of doing anything else but getting where you need to be." That was me. I couldn't think of anything else—we just had to get this paperwork in and move forward quickly.

I received and filled out all the paperwork we needed within a week. We were approved on Wednesday, thirteen days after my answer. I asked our social worker to look over our birth mother letter and scrapbook page to make sure it was okay because we weren't getting a lot of attention at our last agency, and I wanted it to be right.

On Monday, I got a call from our social worker saying that Amy had looked at our birth mother letter and scrapbook page and loved it. I was so relieved that it was okay. She went on to say that Amy wanted to meet us. I thought this was interesting, but not knowing the protocol at the new agency, I said okay. Our social worker said a few more things, until I finally interrupted, "I am so lost as to why Amy wants to meet us."

The social worker said, "She's the birth mother I told you about."

"Ohhhh," I said, "you didn't tell me about any birth mother." An agency is always supposed to tell you about the situation before they show your profile.

When we cleared up the misunderstanding—including the fact that her name was Jamie, not Amy—we learned we were going to have to pay her medical expenses, which would be $7000 more than we were planning on spending. Looking back, we believe it was divine intervention that Jamie saw our profile before we knew about her situation. We are not sure that we would have said yes to having Jamie see our profile because her expenses were so far out of our budget. But Heavenly Father makes things work the way they are supposed to.

I called Mike at work. We were pretty gun shy after what we'd been through. Mike answered that we might as well move forward since she wanted to meet us and then we would see where it went.

We spoke to Jamie two days later on Wednesday. Mike and I were both pretty nervous, and she was too. We talked about her and where she was from. She said she didn't care what religion we were as long as we were religious. She asked us if we belonged to a church and we said, "The Church of Jesus Christ of Latter Day Saints." She was Baptist. Her mother was a minister in her church, and her father was over the youth. She said she sang in the church choir and would sing to the baby all the time. She said she had come to Utah at the beginning of May and that she liked it here but was getting a little homesick to go home to her family. She said she wanted to meet us face-to-face.

We had our face-to-face meeting on that Saturday. We met at a restaurant. I can't express how excited and nervous we were to meet our potential birth mom. It was a quick introduction. The three of us (Mike, Alex, and me) scooted in on one side of the table and Jamie, and two social workers (hers and ours) were across the way.

The one thing I really remember was just staring at Jamie. I finally said to her, "You are *so* beautiful; if your baby looks anything like you, she is going to be so lucky!" Jamie was wearing red, and her hair was pulled back in little braids. She had the most beautiful features. She said the birth father was also very good looking or "hot," as I think she really said. We laughed and said her baby was going to be a lucky little girl.

We decided that we would give Jamie our phone number so she could get in touch with us, and she and I talked a few times over the next few weeks. She told me that she had looked through many profiles and couldn't find one she felt good about, but when ours came in she said, "I just knew it was you. God told me it was you." She also asked me what I was going to tell the baby when she noticed she had darker skin than the rest of us. I said that I would tell her, "Some of us are vanilla and some of us are chocolate, and if you know me at all, you know how much I love chocolate!"

We talked about how to take care of black hair. I didn't know that we would need to perm the baby's hair to make it straighter. Jamie was full African-American, or black; she told me these words were politically correct and interchangeable. She was so kind to help me through some of the stumbling blocks I felt I was falling over.

Jamie told us we needed to get a nursery ready. I told her I was going to wait to make sure everything was okay first. She told me I couldn't wait, and I would have to do it before she'd place the baby with us.

On Tuesday, June 5, we went with Jamie to the doctor. Jamie let us feel the baby kick and move. It was so neat to see Jamie's big round belly! I was so touched that Alex was able to have that experience. It's one of those moments you think about as you have children. You see pictures of moms sitting with their children, sharing the moves and kicks of a sibling, and it was something I felt that I (and Alex) were missing out on—just that bonding with the baby. I was so grateful Jamie allowed us to be able to share that experience with her.

When I first heard the baby's little heart beating, I got all choked up. It was such a beautiful sound. Jamie always told me I cried too much, but she and her baby were so close to my heart that it was difficult not to show my emotions. The doctor said he would start Jamie's labor on June 22.

On the following Monday morning at about 9:00, our social worker called and told us Jamie was in the hospital and that this was it. She was progressing, and they were going to keep her there at the hospital, so we needed to come up. I called Mike at work and said, "You need to come home—we've got a hospital run to make. Jamie's in labor."

Jamie had gone into the hospital around 4:00 AM. We were headed to the hospital around 10:30 AM. It was a somewhat surreal experience driving to the hospital. I wanted to scream, "She's coming! Our baby's coming! We're having a baby!" I was *so* excited and so was Mike.

We were shown to Jamie's room, and while we were waiting, we talked. When her contractions became harder, it was difficult for me to watch since she was helping a baby into this world, and I was going to be able to take the baby home and love her.

Sometime in the afternoon, Mike and I went down to the cafeteria to eat. I caught the doctor in the cafeteria. I was on the phone with my mom and I said to him, "My mom's on the phone, and we'd like to know when the baby will be born because she'd like come up and doesn't want to be too early or too late." The doctor rolled his eyes and said, "Let me think . . . should be around 5:47 PM." *Yeah, right!* I thought.

My parents brought Alex up around 4:00. They sat in the waiting room. Mike and I sat with Jamie and her social worker. At about 5:30 the doctor came in to check her and said it was time to push. Jamie had come all the way from Ohio alone and just had me and her social worker there to help her. I held her hand, and she said she wanted her mom. Her social worker and I looked at each other and both said we hadn't done this part before either, and we both wanted our mothers!

Surprisingly the doctor was only seven minutes off, and at 5:54, our baby arrived. Jamie asked me to cut the umbilical cord. This was all an experience I had never had before. The Spirit was so strong in the room.

Morgan came in weighing only 5 lbs. and 13 oz. and was 18 inches long. She was so small and precious! We just couldn't believe she had arrived. Alex was a proud older brother who had prayed Morgan here for us when we had given up.

As adoption protocol goes, Jamie mothered and I sat back and watched and helped her do it. I tried my best to take care of Jamie, not just because of protocol but because I loved her. She had brought my daughter, Morgan, into this world. I slept in the extra bed in Jamie's room that night. When it was time for Morgan to eat, I took her over to Jamie, and she fed her. When Morgan cried I gave her to Jamie, and then often Jamie would ask me to hold Morgan instead.

At 6 AM on Tuesday, things got a little tough. I was talking about how I had attended BYU—Hawaii. I'm not sure if I said Mormon or if it was because I said "BYU," but suddenly Jamie became very upset. She yelled, "You're a Mormon? You're a Mormon? I'll never be able to attend my little girl's wedding? That's like being a Jehovah's Witness! You're a Mormon!" Jamie was sitting in the chair, and I kneeled on the floor next to her and said, "It's not what you think. We're good people. Our doctrine isn't like the Jehovah Witnesses'. I don't know where Morgan will be in her life when she gets married, but that is up to her, not to us." It was a difficult situation. I thought we were going to lose our Morgan, and I knew if we did I would die!

After fifteen minutes or so, I told Jamie I needed to go out and get a bite to eat, but I immediately went to the waiting room to call Mike. I was sobbing and told him to come up quickly.

I've learned since then that the second day is the hardest for a birth mother—I wish someone had told me that beforehand. I believe that, being a Baptist, the worst thing for Jamie was finding out that we were Mormon *and* that she loved us! That just couldn't be.

Jamie came out to the waiting room and got me. She said she was sorry but that she just couldn't believe I was a Mormon and she really had to think about things. I went back in the room with her, and we watched TV until Mike and then a social worker came. Jamie got on the phone with her case manager, and I told the social worker that Jamie needed to talk about religion. I called our social worker and told her what had happened, and she said she'd be right over. Then I called my mother to come. I wanted to die; I could barely talk; I couldn't eat anything, and I was so sick to my stomach.

After we got back, two case managers went to talk to Jamie. This meeting was at least an hour, and when they came out, the two were arguing. I knew there was big trouble then. I looked at Mike and started sobbing. I immediately got on the phone with my mother and could hardly speak out the words, "Where are you? I need you *now*!" Luckily she was on the first floor, so she came quickly, and I fell into her arms and cried. I just couldn't believe what was happening. In my head I just kept saying, "I can't go home to our freshly painted nursery without a baby. I'll have to burn down the house before I will go in without my daughter!"

After twenty minutes our social worker came out to talk to us. She said that as they were talking, some doctrine about the Mormon

Church had come up. I was just sick. I kept begging to go in and talk to Jamie.

Finally, a third caseworker came out and said Jamie wanted to talk to us. I was so nervous. When we went in, Jamie asked some very difficult doctrinal questions, but I did my best to answer without creating more questions. She asked about hell, she asked about being sealed as a family and where would that leave her, she asked about us being kings and queens in the afterlife.

I then told her how much we loved her. I reminded her about how she had said, "God told me it was you." I reminded her that we hadn't been planning to adopt after our last experience but that God had told us that was a wrong answer. I finally just said, "Jamie, this is between you and God, not you and me, or you and the agency; it's between you and God. He's the only one who can tell you what is right for this baby. You need to talk to him."

We gave Jamie a hug and left the room. A few minutes later, the third social worker came out and said Jamie wanted to talk to us alone. Mike and I went in, and Jamie said that this was the most difficult decision she had ever made but that she was going to go through with the placement and sign the papers the next day. I thanked her and told her how much I loved her and that she was my sister in spirit. Of course, I knew that the next day would be a new day, and I had heard of birth mothers saying they would place and then at the last minute not being able to do it. I wasn't sure Jamie was strong enough to really do it, and I went home feeling very uncertain and scared of what the next day would bring.

The drive home was long. Mike and I could barely talk. What I didn't know was that our entire ward was fasting for us and for Jamie. I believe this is what eventually led Jamie to sign the papers. One convert sister in our ward wanted to grab all the sisters in our ward and go to the hospital right then to talk to Jamie and let her know how good of a family we were and how much better off her she and her baby would be. It still makes me teary thinking of all the support our ward family and my Relief Society sisters gave to us.

When I arrived home, within five minutes there were three adoptive moms and my next-door neighbor at my doorstep. I think they were waiting and watching for us. They all gave me the strength to go on. My mom was there too and made sure we were all taken care of.

Someone had dropped lasagna off, and my mom had fixed that for all of us to eat. It tasted so good, and I was so grateful for that service.

That night Mike, Alex, and I all got into our king-size bed. I don't usually sleep well with anyone in my bed, especially three of us. But we all fell instantly asleep and slept that way all night. I must say it was so nice to wake up with our family together and feel the strength we had for each other. We all wanted our fourth family member so much.

Mike, Alex, and I went up to the hospital about 9:00 AM with complete trepidation. We were nervous about what was about to transpire. I felt like a walking zombie. We saw Jamie for a moment or two, and then we went down to eat. My heart was heavy for Jamie; we were all solemn and quiet.

We gave Jamie a necklace with a pearl inside gold loops. The loops curved in and around each other, and we said we felt like it was her and Morgan entwined forever as birth mother and daughter. While we were there, Jamie asked me what I would do if Morgan had to stay one more night in the hospital. I said I'd stay right there by the baby; Jamie was relieved by my answer. The day was long, and it took a long time for them to go over the paperwork with Jamie. It was so difficult for her to sign because she loved Morgan so much and wanted to be with her.

Around 2:30 PM they took us into an extra room, and about a half hour later Jamie left, and they brought Morgan into us. You should have seen the tears of joy. We were all so relieved because we knew she was part of our family and that Jamie had made the difficult choice and followed Heavenly Father's promptings.

Morgan did end up spending another night in the hospital. But it was a nice night for me because I was able to spend some time alone with her, since I knew there would be a few people coming to visit as soon as we went home.

The nurses were kind enough to give me an empty room at the end of the hallway where I could take Morgan and sleep on a bed there. After everyone was gone that night, I laid by Morgan on the bed and watched every move she made. I told her over and over how much I loved her and how happy we were that she had come into our lives. It was a little hard for me to believe she was really laying there beside me—all 5 lbs. and 13 oz. of her. It was a moment I had waited for since Alex was tiny. I just couldn't wait to get her home and take care of her. I had thought about this moment for six years and now that it was really, truly here, it was hard for me to believe!

The next day we were able to go home. It was such a thrill. My mom said I needed to keep our new baby away from people because she was so little. But I said, "Just how do you plan on me doing that when the entire ward has prayed and fasted to get her here?"

When we arrived at home, our garage was completely decorated with yellow and pink balloons and a huge sign that read, "Welcome Home, Morgan." (I heard that they had put it up when they heard Morgan had arrived, then taken it down when Jamie was upset, and finally put it back up when the papers were signed. We had tape marks all over our garage!) We were just getting out of the car when all the neighbors came running out. Then word traveled quickly. It was like a huge ward party at our home that night.

I will never get over how the Lord's hand worked in our behalf. People sometimes tell me that we saved Morgan, but it isn't that way at all—she saved us.

11

NELS & AMBER'S STORY

Fred Riley, commissioner of LDS Family Services, says that although adoption is rarely discussed in Church meetings, it is a profound gospel principle. He points out that when the prophet Elijah restored the sealing keys, these keys encompassed adoption. And one of the ways in which Jesus Christ is our Father is through adoption, for we become His sons and His daughters when we are adopted into the family of Christ. . . . "From the time of Adam, adoption has been a priesthood ordinance," says Brother Riley. "It's a principle of the gospel that probably all of us will experience at some point as we're literally adopted into our Heavenly Father's kingdom."

—*Rebecca M. Taylor*[13]

My family's story starts when I was a young girl. I dreamed that my family had an African-American child, a Hispanic child, and an Asian child. When I started dating my husband, I would point out all the beautiful children and tell him that I wanted one of them. His response was always, "That isn't possible because we're both white."

We got married, and although we had talked about waiting at least a year before having children, within one month we both felt strongly that we had to start trying to have a family. So we did, and each month was devastating as we discovered we were not pregnant. After six months I felt in my heart of hearts that we would be adopting. I started looking at adoption seriously, but LDS Family Services (LDSFS) has a rule that you have to be married for two years.

At one year we went to the ob-gyn and found out that it would be a medical miracle if we were to ever conceive a biological child. At that point I was so excited because it meant that the family of my dreams could come true. My husband was not so sure he wanted to adopt transracially because it would be so different. I went over to one of my friend's apartment and ran into a girl that I had known three years earlier in my BYU ward. She was a social worker with an agency in Utah, and she gave me her card. I promptly put the card in my car's cup holder and forgot about it.

We went to LDSFS in August, before our two-year mark, and had all the paperwork filled out and turned in on December 21, our second anniversary. Then they proceeded to lose our papers, frustrate us, and otherwise drive us away. Looking back we can see that this was all part of the plan. If we had not been frustrated, then we would probably still be waiting with them because we would not have known about any other options, and, as it turned out, our baby was not with LDSFS.

After a particularly hard day, while we were still waiting with LDSFS, I pulled into my garage, and there was the card from my old friend—still in my cup holder six months after she gave it to me. I went inside and told my husband that we needed to call this agency. He called and found out about their programs and that they specifically worked with African-American adoptions.

At that time (January 2007) I had a very strong impression that our baby was here and we needed to get everything done quickly for our baby. We got the paperwork done and were ready to turn it in on their first meeting of the year. At that meeting was a beautiful family that had adopted transracially with two beautiful boys. That family is the reason my husband decided that we needed to adopt an African-American baby.

We turned in our paperwork for only an African-American or a biracial child. The Spirit was so strong at that meeting, even when a family stood up and talked about a baby they'd had in their care but had lost due to birth-father rights. After the meeting, I knew that this was the agency that our baby would come through. But then it took the state of Utah three months to get my fingerprints back—something that agency had never seen before.

In the meantime two different babies were offered to us that were not African-American and that had legal fees attached to them that we could not afford. As much as I cried each time, they were not our babies. We got officially approved to adopt in April 2007 and then heard nothing until July, when we were called about a possibly biracial baby girl. But we turned the adoption down. It was the perfect time: in the summer, when I was not teaching. It was the perfect situation: a baby girl, who was very light skinned. But she was not our baby.

That time the crying and worrying and feeling that this adoption was not going to happen lasted a lot longer, but we knew through the Spirit that this was not our baby and that our time was not the Lord's time. However, we felt that we needed to get a little extra money in our bank account in case the right situation was just outside our budget, so we took a credit card cash advance.

Then right in the middle of our opening faculty meeting for school, I got a phone call that there was birth mother in Kentucky who wanted to see our profile. The person on the phone asked if we would like our profile to be sent and told me that the baby was not expected until early September. We said yes but did not expect to hear anything more since nothing had happened every other time. The next day, just after a district-wide meeting, I got a phone call that said a baby girl had been born in Kentucky at 5:00 AM and that the birth mother wanted a family that could be there as soon as possible. I said yes immediately, without even knowing how much it would cost. I called my husband at work, and he proceeded to get plane tickets leaving at 5:00 PM and a rental car. I told my principal that I would be gone for at least the first week of school and that our baby had been born. I then ran home to pack and leave. We needed to bring a check with us to pay for the adoption, so we stopped at the bank and walked out of the building with $1,000—our adoption cost exactly the amount we had in our bank account.

We flew out to Kentucky and met the most amazing woman I have ever known. We talked over speakerphone with our daughter's birth grandmother and then finally got to meet our beautiful baby girl. The first time my husband held her in his arms, he knew that she was our baby. She is the most beautiful African-American/Hispanic little girl.

Of course she was born in August—eight months after I had felt that our baby was here and that we needed to go get her. The feeling I had happened right when my daughter's birth mother would have found out she was expecting this angel.

Without the miracle of adoption, two very white people like us could never have had such an amazing baby in our lives. Ten months later we got to take our daughter to the temple, the day after we finalized her adoption and the day before we left Utah to start a new adventure in the east. While in the temple, my husband felt the spirit of his deceased mother and knew that she was there with us. Then when we blessed our daughter, his father handed him a letter, written before his mother passed away. The letter said she would try to be present at all our happy moments, and this was one of our happiest.

12

Mat & Shelly's Story

We . . . express our support of unwed parents who place their children for adoption in stable homes with a mother and a father. We also express our support of the married mothers and fathers who adopt these children. Children are entitled to the blessing of being reared in a stable family environment where father and mother honor marital vows. Having a secure, nurturing, and consistent relationship with both a father and a mother is essential to a child's well-being. When choosing adoption, unwed parents grant their children this most important blessing. Adoption is an unselfish, loving decision that blesses the child, birth parents, and adoptive parents in this life and throughout the eternities. We commend all those who strengthen children and families by promoting adoption.

—First Presidency statement[14]

Just a little about us: my husband, Mat, and I have been married almost twenty-three years and have five biological children who are Caucasian and two adopted daughters who are African-American. We have one son and six daughters. Tanner is twenty and serving a mission in Indonesia. Sara, 19, just returned from five months in China teaching English. Our other daughters are Katie, fifteen; Chloe, eight;

Meg and Mati, who are both seven but not twins; and Halle who is one. Mat is a regional director for a software company, and I work with Heart to Heart Adoptions doing public relations work from home. Mat loves all sports and is an avid reader. He is an amazing father, the life of the party everywhere we go, and he makes everything fun. I enjoy music, art, baking, and just being with my family.

There is obviously a big space between Katie (child number three) and Chloe (child number four). We tried for several years to have another child, but it never happened. Then we babysat a friend's recently adopted baby over a weekend, and our fate was sealed. We wanted to adopt! As fate would have it, about the time we had our papers together, we learned I was pregnant. It was a very difficult pregnancy, starting with a PICC line (peripherally inserted central catheter) and ending with a C-section.

We still wanted to adopt. We were prayerful during our entire journey. There were quite a few bumps along the way, including a cancer scare with Mat. He had a cough that wouldn't go away, so he went for a CT scan, and it showed some weird spots. They thought it was probably cancer. Long and anxiety-ridden story short, it was not. It was desert fever, a fungus that can grow in the lungs. But while he was sick and being treated, I never stopped pressing forward with the adoption process. I would pull all-nighters getting paperwork together, assembling a profile, and doing research, research, research on everything I could. At one point my dad said, "Are you just thinking you want to raise five kids alone instead of four?" It seemed harsh, but he had a point. Even so, I just couldn't or wouldn't stop. I knew we were to adopt.

All along the way, I felt all the emotions that potential adoptive parents feel: apprehension, anxiety, fear, excitement. But I also had an underlying peace that kept me going. The only thing I struggled with consistently was my own ability to receive an answer to prayer—specifically, how would we know which birth mom or situation was supposed to be ours?

People would tell me, "Oh, you'll just *know*." But that seemed a little vague, to say the least, and I guess I didn't have much faith. Or at least enough faith that I would *know*. We were being told about so many birth moms so quickly, I just felt nervous that I wouldn't recognize ours. And at one point, the agency worker said, "Oh, I just feel so inspired this is your situation." (Incidentally, it wasn't.) But her comment made me *mad*! I didn't feel that it was her privilege to receive inspiration for me or my family.

I was praying, fasting, reading my scriptures, trying to be a good mom, taking care of my husband who didn't feel well, and trying to sort through the physical and emotional demands of navigating an adoption. In short, my world was chaos. I craved peace. I craved the comforting presence of the Holy Ghost. And I wanted and needed help in knowing which situation would be right for us. We had prayerfully made the decision to adopt, but the next step was *who*? Which birth mom was ours?

I decided to go to the temple, but not to ask for a vision, revelation, or even an answer. I had heard about the amazing experiences people have in the temple; seeing loved ones who had gone on before, or running into a person there whose influence was needed, who just happened to be in the same session. And while I am sure those experiences have happened for others, honestly they never had for me. I had felt peace and learned things at the temple, but I hadn't ever really had anything profound happen. I don't really consider myself to be a spiritual dynamo; I am not a great scriptorian, nor am I what some would refer to as a gospel scholar. I am a daughter, sister, wife, and mom who has a testimony of Heavenly Father and Jesus Christ, and I try to be a disciple. I try to serve others and love unconditionally. I try to be a good wife and mom and want nothing more than to be with my family through eternity. I guess you could say I am just a regular person!

But the stress of life, particularly this decision, was weighing heavily on me. The phone was ringing off the hook (okay, a few times a day, but it felt like off the hook) with potential adoption situations. Our paperwork wasn't even complete, and we were getting calls. We didn't have our financing in place, even if the right birth mom did come along. Yet I felt driven and compelled to keep things moving. I was also becoming exhausted and feeling overwhelmed and tense. I just wanted an escape. I needed a break. And while heading to Hawaii sounded perfectly rational to me, I opted to go spend a day in the Jordan River Temple. My mom was a key person in the Jordan River Temple dedication (she prepared and served all the meals for the First Presidency and General Authorities during the dedication ceremonies) and in addition to being able to help her and her amazing group of sisters from our stake, I was given the opportunity to play the organ for several sessions during the open house. I was only fourteen at the time, and it was a special experience for me. Ever since then, the Jordan River Temple has held a special spot in my heart. I got a babysitter for an entire day and told Mat I was unavailable and was going to the temple for the day.

My patriarchal blessing counsels me that "when there are . . . confusing situations you do not understand and need guidance, go quickly to your Father in Heaven in humble prayer on your knees and he will give you understanding and peace in your heart, and you may have a sweet spirit of love and harmony and peace in your home. . . . I bless you with patience and perseverance that you may realize the eternal nature of your responsibilities."

My purpose in going to the temple was not to receive a revelation, vision, or visitation. I didn't even want an answer to anything. I wanted peace. I wanted to be surrounded by complete peace and love and, in a literal way, to leave the world outside. I didn't want to hear or answer the phone. I didn't want to see the computer staring at me, feeling like I should keep researching, reading, or writing. And I needed a break from being a caretaker—just a temporary break—and I knew that being inside the sacred walls of the temple, I would make the shift from being a caretaker to being cared for by Heavenly Father. In fact, I decided that the prayer in my heart would just be that I would have faith enough to recognize the answer when I received it. And faith to move forward when that happened.

So, with all arrangements made, I happily headed to my day of rest—my entire day at the temple. I decided I'd either just repeat sessions, one after the other, or participate in different ordinances throughout the day. I also hoped to just be able to sit in the celestial room and ponder. I needed to rest spiritually, physically, and emotionally.

I began the first of what I thought would be many sessions during the day at around 9 AM. As it began, I said a quiet prayer, just asking Heavenly Father to let me feel peace and calm and to help me know that he would be with me through this process of adopting. I asked him to help me know when the right birth mom came along. I settled into my chair and instantly felt a deep sense of calm and complete release. I felt my body and mind completely relax and felt very much that all I needed to remember were the words "be still and know that

I am God." And I was filled with peace.

By the end of the session, I was tranquil and happy. As a prayer was offered, the words "bless those who have come to the temple with a prayer in their hearts, that their prayer will be answered and the worthy desires of their hearts fulfilled," made a lasting impression on my mind. I became emotional and felt this was meant specifically for me. And right then, I knew that our birth mother's name was Tia. I have never known anyone before or since with that name, but it was almost as if the words were spoken to me: "Your birth mother is Tia." I didn't even have a cause to wonder. It was so clear, and I did not doubt for a minute or rethink it. I just about ran out of the temple that day. I had planned to spend the day there and wanted so desperately to just sit in the celestial room as long as I wanted. But I didn't. I didn't even sit down. I went straight out, changed into my street clothing, and literally ran to my car. I called Mat and said, "I know our birth mother's name!" I rattled off how it had happened, and told him that I was not nervous, and I was not doubtful. *I just knew.*

A few days later when I was talking to an agency representative, she mentioned the need for maternity clothing for the birth moms. I had a one-year-old and plenty of maternity clothes. I offered to bring mine to her home to donate to the birth mothers that night. She said that night was not good because she was picking up a new birth mother—Tawanna—from the airport. But she asked if I could come the next day. I agreed. The box was large, and Chloe was not quite a year old yet, so I enlisted Mat's help. He agreed to come help me unload the boxes, but he had to get back to work when he could. We took the older kids to school and went to drop off the box of clothing.

When we arrived, a few birth mothers were there, and some kids were running around. We dragged our big box in, and I noticed one particular birth mother standing against a wall, kind of away from the group. She was pretty quiet, but I thought very beautiful. She had all her hair slicked back in a high bun, and she had big beautiful eyes. We introduced ourselves to each birth mother: Taquia, Dorothy, Shanny, and Tawanna. We shook hands with each one and then moved to the next one. When we got to the last woman, I said, "Hi, I'm Shelly." She smiled widely—her trademark as I later came to find out—and said, "Hey, I'm Tawanna—you can call me Tia".

Well, as you can imagine, I started to shake. My heart started racing, and my eyes filled with tears. Her name was TIAwanna, but with her thick Georgia accent, we all thought it was Tawanna! I excused myself to attempt composure, and when I pulled it together and returned to the group, Mat had left! So again, I excused myself and called Mat. I was hissing into my cell phone, "Where did you go? What are you doing? That is our birth mother!" Mat said, "I know. That's why I left. I knew as soon as I saw her standing away from the group."

I again attempted to compose myself and went back into the room. All the birth mothers were gone, except Tia. We chatted very superficially, and she asked if Chloe was my only child. I laughed and told her, "No, I have three others who are in school." She said, "Wow, that's a lotta kids. You gonna have more?" I told her no, we didn't think I could have anymore. She asked if I'd considered adopting before. I told her absolutely and that I was hoping to very soon, actually. She said, "I think you should adopt my baby." I said, "I would love to!" It was as simple as that.

And then she said, "I'm starved. How 'bout you?" (Uh, does it matter? I am always up for a meal!) So we decided to go to lunch. She was pretty fussy about too much mayo, not enough mustard, pickles were soft—there was nothing very pleasing to her in that sandwich. And I dutifully responded, jumping up and running to the counter, requesting the changes. (I later found out the two agency friends who were with me laughed long and hard about me jumping up and down and just doing everything to keep her happy! It would be a pattern that continued for a few months.)

We went back to the house she was staying at, and I asked if she wanted to see my profile—which I had just completed and was going to leave there along with the maternity clothes. She looked at it and said, "I knew you were the one when you walked in the room, and as soon as I shook your husband's hand."

We had a great last trimester with Tia and ran it as a private adoption. We were lucky to have great support from friends and family. Tia spent time in our home and went to our children's activities with us. She cooked soul food for us one night, and we cooked crepes for her because she said she'd never had them. She braided Sara and Katie's hair, and we had a great relationship with her.

One of my favorite memories is when we were first getting to know each other, I said something about her being "African-American." She interrupted me and said, "Look, Miss Shelly. I ain't from Africa. I didn't come over here on a boat. Neither did my parents or grandparents. I am black; you are white. You raise this baby to be a strong black woman." I loved that!

Originally, Tia didn't want to see or hold the baby. She said she knew "what happens when you hold a new baby," and she wanted that bond to be between the baby and me. Delivery was quite an event. I had all scheduled C-sections, so I had never even been in labor. That meant this was the first "real" delivery Mat and I had seen. I kept getting dizzy and had to sit down, so everyone had to take a break every time I got sick. I couldn't believe I was such a wuss! I had worked in hospitals and doctor's offices and had assisted in surgeries, yet I was getting ill at the delivery of my own baby.

Meg's arrival was the most amazing thing I have ever seen. Mat cut the cord, and I was just in awe of the miracle that had occurred and Tia's complete selflessness in going through that, then giving that sweet, perfect baby to me. Our children joined us a few hours after delivery, and we all gave Meg her first bath together. I slept at the hospital that night. The hospital was gracious enough to give me an extra room, and I slept with Meg curled up in my arms all night. I woke up around 3:00 AM. I wasn't startled, but I felt someone looking at me. Tia was sitting in a chair at the foot of my bed. I asked, "Tia, are you okay?" and she just smiled and said, "I just need to see you falling in love." We spent the twenty-four hours after delivery together at the hospital, and I was able to "trick" Tia into holding Meg (in a good way). I have photos of that, and it was a great moment.

Three days after delivery, we had a farewell party at our house for Tia, and then she went back home to Georgia. Before she left for the airport, I left her and Meg in my bedroom alone and told her to take all the time she needed to say good-bye to Meg. She only took about fifteen minutes, and then she came out of the bedroom. She always told us how much she loved us—all of us—and when she was ready to go, she hugged me, and with tears streaming down her face, she said, "Tell Meg I loved her enough to give her to you." I cherish that memory, and I am so grateful I have this to share with Meg.

Meg had some trouble her first few months with clonus and reflux. At about three weeks of age, she was admitted to Primary Children's to find out to find out why she had tremors and screamed 24/7. It was determined that Tia must have used some drugs while pregnant.

That Saturday was conference weekend, and I was worn out and just didn't feel well. I went to get my blood work done to find out if something serious was wrong, but I just wrote it off to the exhaustion and stress from the adoption. That afternoon Meg was discharged from the hospital, and it was almost time for the priesthood session of conference. I was raised that you encourage men (okay, *force* them, if necessary) to go to the general priesthood session. No exceptions! That's where they need to be, and they come home better from it. But that night, I was hanging on by a thread. I was so sick, so exhausted, and I said, "Mat, I can't do it alone tonight." Chloe was a busy one-year-old, Meg was a very fussy newborn, plus I had three elementary-age children who needed me. I asked him to stay home—just this once. I think he was so surprised that I would ask him to miss, he thought I must be dying or something. Later that evening, maybe 8:30 or 9, when the priesthood session was clearly over, our phone rang. The caller ID said "NELSON, RUSSELL M." I saw that and said, "I'm not answering! I knew you should have gone to priesthood!" Mat answered, and I heard him talk for a moment. The he handed the phone to me. He said, "This one's for you." It was Dr. Irion (Elder Nelson's son-in-law). The lab had called his home and Gloria, his wife, had called him. As soon as priesthood was over, Dr. Irion had gone to Elder Nelson's house for dinner or something, and from there he had called the lab to confirm his suspicion: I was definitely pregnant. Again, I had three elementary kids, a busy one-year-old, and a very fussy three-week-old . . . and now I was pregnant! Dr Irion was awesome. He just told me that this must be a very special spirit and that this was just another adventure.

We spoke with Tia two or three times that first year and haven't heard from her again. She wanted it this way. I think she just needed to know Meg was with her family, and then she wanted to move on. Meg *is* with her family. Just the way Heavenly Father planned her to be.

13

JEREMY & LYNDSEY'S STORY

We know that activity in the Church centers in the family.
Wherever members are in the world, they should establish a family
where children are welcome and treasured as "an heritage of the Lord"
(Psalm 127:3). A worthy Latter-day Saint family is a standard to
the world.

—*Boyd K. Packer*[15]

My adoption journey began in June of 2004. I delivered a beautiful baby girl that month. Yes, some people who choose to adopt have also delivered a child at some point. Everything went so right during the delivery, or so I thought. I remember having chest pains under my left breast and asking the nurse about them. She just passed it off as a hole in the epidural. Later on I would come to find out I had a developed a condition during my delivery called Peripartum Cardiomyopathy.

My heart had enlarged and was not working properly anymore. Many doctor's visits and a healthy amount of medication later, I was good to go. But I was told that if I ever got pregnant again, my chances of dying were 50 percent. Not willing to risk leaving my husband a widower just to have another child, we knew adoption was the next step.

We signed up for the adoption classes and began the long journey of completing our paperwork and home study. We waited with LDS Family Services for about a year and a half, and then I knew it was time to move on. I knew my baby was out there, waiting to be born, and I needed to change agencies. It was like we were being guided by the Lord as to what we needed to do.

The night we found out about our baby, we were already planning to go to the temple. The agency told us about our birth mom and asked us to let them know in the next couple of days if we thought this was a match. On the drive to the temple, we giggled the whole way there and talked quickly like we were in high school again. The couple we went with probably thought we were nuts. I have never been one of those people who get an answer to every prayer, but when we asked about our baby, it was a definite yes! I have never felt so sure about anything in my entire life.

Our families were not at all supportive of our decision to adopt an African-American child, but their worries were founded on ignorance and fear. We were going to adopt this child, with or without their blessing. About five weeks later, our birth mother went into labor, and we booked tickets to Virginia. We found out just before we left that it was false labor, but we decided to go anyway.

A week later we had hit all the hot spots in Virginia and were starting to get a little bit freaked out by the waiting. But then she finally went into real labor. It was a boy! Some moments will forever be burned into your memory, and the birth of both of my children is a memory I will never forget. We were told to go to the hospital two days later and pick up our little bundle of joy.

When we arrived, we were told the birth mother needed another hour to sign the relinquishment papers and that we should go for a walk to give her time. So we walked around the hospital and found a cemetery to walk through. It was a quiet time between husband and wife where nothing had to be said because we both understood how the other was feeling and what the other was thinking.

We never knew our birth mother, and that was a choice she made. We chose to honor and respect her painful decision. The first time we saw Elijah was in the hallway at the hospital. His big eyes stared up at us, and his little brows had a questioning look on them. He was the most beautiful baby boy I had ever seen. We didn't dare touch him for fear this dream would be taken away.

Our biggest concern at that moment was wondering if we would try to walk out of the hospital only to have someone stop us and tell us we were stealing this baby. The lawyer assured us he was ours and that no one was going to stop us. On the way back to our timeshare, our daughter looked over at Elijah and said, "Dad, be careful. We have a baby in the car." A week later we left Virginia to start our life again and to be forever grateful for the choice of a beautiful daughter of God.

14

JONATHAN & TRISHA'S STORY

We believe in being honest, true, chaste, benevolent, virtuous, and in doing good to all men; indeed, we may say that we follow the admonition of Paul—We believe all things, we hope all things, we have endured many things, and hope to be able to endure all things. If there is anything virtuous, lovely, or of good report of praiseworthy, we seek after these things.

—Articles of Faith 1:13

My name is Trisha, and my husband is Jonathan. When we began the adoption process, we already had one biological daughter, Courtney, who was born in 1996, but because of infertility issues, we felt we should start the process, and so we chose to go through LDS Family Services (LDSFS) in the fall of 2000. We were approved in the spring of 2001 and began the waiting process. Unbeknownst to us, our son was born in Orem, Utah, on May 10, 2001. It would be eight and a half months before we would welcome him into our home. We waited and waited and basically had little to no activity on our profile. I became frustrated over all of the waiting, but time did pass rather quickly because there were so many things going on in our personal lives. I was in the middle of graduate school, working on my masters of education, my father passed away in the summer of 2001 from leukemia, and we had to move my mom away from my childhood home and help her get through all the firsts without my dad. For example, the first missed anniversary, all of the missed birthdays, Thanksgiving, and Christmas. I also returned to work full-time as a teacher. I had originally gone back to work part-time, teaching high school, even as I hoped for a pregnancy and adding another child to our family.

Shortly after Christmas of 2001, we invited my mother over for dinner, and she sat us down to have a little talk. She wanted to offer the financial help we needed that would allow us to pursue other adoption options, like going through a private adoption agency. My mom had a lot of empathy for us, considering she had walked in our shoes in the late 1960s. She had also dealt with infertility, and adoption was the choice my parents had made. Thankfully things worked out for them, and I have my brother and sister. I was the surprise pregnancy that came after their adoptions. Nevertheless, my mother knew how my heart ached to have more children.

We immediately started to search for an agency. In a matter of a few weeks we were working with The Adoption Center of Choice in Orem, Utah. Since our profile was put together for LDSFS and our home study complete, we were able to transfer those items to our new agency, and therefore, we were in a position to be immediately shown to birth mothers. I took all the necessary paperwork to this new agency on Martin Luther King Day in January 2002. By Friday night of that same week, there was a little girl that had been born and needed surgery at Primary Children's hospital for a minor hernia. Her birth mother had chosen a family in Canada, but due to the additional medical expenses, that family was unable to take the baby girl. The agency called us, but we did not have the feeling that this was our little girl.

Up to this point, I had always felt like I would be ready for the first baby that was offered to us from a birth mother. I had friends who had already gone through the adoption process, and they tried to help me understand that I would know deep in my heart when we were matched with the child that was meant for our family. I never placed much value in this thought because I so desperately wanted another child. When we were presented with this first situation from this agency, we prayed about it, and neither my husband nor I felt like we had received any sort of confirmation that we were supposed to pursue this baby girl. My heart ached, and I shed many tears over this decision, but when it came right down to it, she was not our baby.

Less than a week later, the next Thursday, I received another call from the agency. They told us about a situation involving an eight-and-a-half-month-old little African-American boy. She told me that this little boy had been originally placed by his birth mother with a family in Arizona. The first adoptive mother, Christy, called the agency on Wednesday, January 30, and asked for their help. She began to describe her situation to the agency. They were members of the Church and had recently adopted three children. They were a fairly young couple, and all three of their children had come into their family through separate adoptions, and all within a two-year span. The oldest child was two at the time the youngest son was born.

The actual truth of what happened was never really revealed to us, but it is my theory the husband felt overwhelmed at the circumstances they found themselves in. Sometime during the holiday season, he decided to leave his wife and their three children. Christy was devastated. Sometime in early January she was driving down the road and heard a voice as clear as day. Being a member of the Church throughout her life, she knew it was the Spirit speaking to her. Obviously, she was in tune, and thank goodness she was. Otherwise we might not have Ammon in our family today. She pulled over on the side of the road and prayed, cried, and pleaded with her Heavenly Father.

The prompting Christy heard in her car that day told her to ask for help with Ammon, her youngest child. The voice told her she needed to ask the agency to help re-place Ammon with another family. She was devastated, and for the next few weeks she didn't do anything about it. Eventually, she couldn't deny what she had heard that day, and she asked her family for help. She then called the agency, and they told her they would be able to place Ammon again. The following day (Thursday, January 31), Christy's father flew to Salt Lake and relinquished custody of Ammon to the agency.

The very day the agency took back custody, they called us because we were basically the only family immediately ready for placement, since our home study was completed. They said we could come see Ammon and take temporary custody of him to see if this was the right match. I knew that if I saw him first, of course I would want him—no matter what my head said. If we decided to take Ammon, he would not have to go into any type of transitional care until a match could be found. When I received the phone call, I explained to the agency that my husband and I had to have the confirmation of the Spirit to know if this was the right match. They agreed, and so I went to my husband's work and explained the situation to him. Without hesitation he said, "We are not going to see him, we are going to go get him!" I broke down in tears and hugged Jon. At that moment I knew in my heart that this was our baby boy.

I frantically made some phone calls and began to organize some things while Jon finished work for the day. As soon as he could get away from work, we were on our way to Orem to meet our son. By seven that same night, we were back in Salt Lake, introducing our new son to our extended family. This whole process was a bit of a whirlwind. The story does have a bit more to it, as I was eventually able to have a conversation with Christy. She personally shared her spiritual experience with me. I also have my own reasons for believing Ammon was always meant to be in our family, but due to the personal challenges we faced during the summer and fall of 2001, the Lord knew Ammon needed to temporarily be with another family to receive the love and care Christy and her family gave him. I truly believe the Lord knew when the right time was to have Ammon come join our family.

15

MATT & SUSAN'S STORY

If you live up to your privileges, the angels cannot be restrained from being your associates.

—*Joseph Smith*[16]

My name is Susan, and I have adopted two little girls, one who is African-American and one who is Caucasian. They are both beautiful, and I have amazing stories for both of them, but here I will share my story of Sophie, my little black angel.

My husband, Matt, and I were blessed to be able to have a beautiful baby boy after trying for three long years. Since we knew fertility was a struggle for us, we tried almost nonstop to have another baby. Almost seven years went by, and still it was just the three of us. At that time, it felt right to start the adoption process. We began our journey through LDS Family Services (LDSFS) and took all our classes. It was a great place to start because the Spirit was definitely with us through this experience. I always knew in the back of my mind that I wanted to adopt a black child, but whenever I brought the subject up with my husband, he would get this look of panic on his face.

At that time, I decided to let the race of our child go while we focused on finishing all of our classes. Our next assignment was to finish

83

all of our paperwork, write our birth mother letter, and put together some pictures of our family. Every time I sat down to do this, I felt as if I were writing an advertisement for myself, like, "Pick me! I would be the best mom *ever* for your child!" I couldn't do it. I knew I had so much to give a child, but to actually have to write it down was extremely difficult for me. So I just put it aside and tried not to think about it.

It was then that I started having a recurring dream. It wasn't a dream of a beautiful black child or anything like that. It was a strange dream where all I could see were words being said to me. Every time I had a dream I was told, *There is a little girl that is going to be born soon. Get ready.*

One morning I woke up after having this dream again, and the phone rang. It was my mom, and she said, "I don't want you to get mad or anything, but I have to tell you about this dream I had last night." I just said okay, and she said, "There is a little girl that has been born or is going to born soon, and you need to get ready." I didn't tell her I was having the same dream; I just said something like, "Oh really? Okay, Mom." But when I hung up with her, the panic really set in. I knew I couldn't do anything about adopting a child until I had everything in order and had completed my home study, which included that birth mother letter. At this point, writing the letter felt like a hopeless task.

I knew I needed help, so I called a friend of mine and asked her if she would go to the temple with me the next day. I knew I needed to do some serious praying. I needed peace, and the temple felt like the perfect place to find it. And of course it was. It was early February and it was cold, but the sun was so bright. We chose to go to the Bountiful Temple. When we got inside the temple, we split up. I had told my friend that I needed to be by myself for a little while so I could communicate with the Spirit. I went and sat by a window, facing the sun so I could feel the warmth on my face. I bowed my head and had a wonderful talk with my Heavenly Father about some of my concerns. I told Heavenly Father that I needed his help to get this paperwork done. I asked that he would give me the strength and courage to write this letter.

The next day I sat down to write my letter, and the same overwhelming weaknesses fell over me again. I didn't know what to do. So again I just put it aside. A couple hours later, my phone rang. A woman asked, "Is this Susan?" And I said yes. She said, "This is Maureen from the adoption classes. I was just calling to see how your paperwork is going." Maureen was a girl I had met through LDSFS.

I remember just looking up and thinking, *Okay, I get it, Heavenly Father. I will get the letter done. Thanks for answering my prayer.* I started laughing and told Maureen about my problem and how I had just been to the temple the day before. I told her that I knew she was sent to help me. Maureen said she had just picked up her adoption folder and my name fell out of the book and that she had just felt inspired to call me. I am so glad she followed that inspiration. She told me to call LDSFS after we hung up to make the appointment, so then I would be on a time schedule to get everything done.

I did. After I made the appointment, I only had two weeks to get everything finished. With a lot of prayer and blessings, I was able to write my letter. We had our home study, and our caseworker called a couple of weeks later to tell us that we had been approved. But then came what we thought would be the harder part—the wait. Where was this little girl we had all these strong feelings about?

We had a big family get-together the weekend after we got the call that we were approved. My aunt was there, and I told her that we had just been approved through LDSFS. We talked about it for a few minutes, and she became really excited for our family.

The following Thursday my aunt called and said she had a friend that had an adoption agency in Ogden. That agency had a little girl who was five weeks old and available for adoption in Las Vegas. They had not been able to place her. If I was interested, my aunt told me I should give her friend a call. So I called and got all the information. When my husband came home, I ran out to tell him about the news, but I didn't know how to tell him she was a little black baby or how much it was going to cost because I knew that would be his first question. So all I said was, "My aunt called. She says there is a five-week-old baby girl in Las Vegas, ready to be adopted right now."

And the first thing he said was, "How much?"

I replied, "You can't put a price tag on a baby."

He said, "Yes, I can. We can't afford to go through one of these expensive agencies."

I quickly shot back that the Spirit was telling me that this was our baby. I said, "Let's just put our faith in Heavenly Father that he will take care of this and help us find a way."

Then his next question was, "What color?"

I said African-American and then the look came again.

"I don't know if I can do it" was his response.

I replied, "I don't know, honey. I just don't know." Then I said, "I know I'm scared to death too."

It was a rough night that night. Neither one of us could hold still, and there were a lot of looks exchanged, but I was afraid if I kept talking about it, he would get fed up with me and just say no. The next morning Matt went off to work and said not to call the agency because he needed more time to think about it. I said okay, but at eight in the morning, the phone rang, and it was the adoption agency. They said the adoption was being put together; it felt like I had no control over the whole thing. It was happening.

Looking back, it was so surreal. I didn't know what to do. I was there in my kitchen with the phone ringing off the hook. The agency kept telling me all the things they needed from me, and I didn't want to send them anything because my husband had told me a few hours before that he needed more time. I knew I couldn't do any of this without Matt, so it got to the point where I had to call him and tell him what was happening.

When I called Matt, he told me to just tell them no and that this was not going to happen. But I told him I didn't want to do that. He would have to tell them this adoption was not going to work. At that point, I was so emotional that I needed him to come home. So much was happening, and even if we decided this was not right, I needed him home. So he came home and got on the phone with the agency. But he couldn't say the words either. He just couldn't do it.

When he hung up, he said, "I need to call the bishop." I never heard the conversation, but when he got off the phone with the bishop, he said, "I think I need a blessing. Will you call your dad?" So I did. My mom and dad came over, and my dad and Matt gave me a blessing first, and then my dad gave Matt a blessing. A few seconds into the blessing, I had one of the most spiritual experiences of my life. It was as if the living room just opened up and was filled with spirits. I didn't recognize most of them, but there were a lot of spirits there, and in the blessing the Spirit said that it was preordained that Matt was supposed to be the father of this blessed baby and that she was meant to be with him.

For the first time since the whole adoption process had began, I saw a peace come over Matt, and when the blessing was over, with tears in his eyes, he said, "Let's get ready to go get our little girl." We called the agency, and they said, "Everything is in order, except we need you to talk with the birth mother because she wants to be involved with who we place this baby with."

They gave me a list of things I could not talk to her about. Two of the big ones were race and religion. We were so scared. What if we messed this up and ended up not getting this baby? I called her and the first thing she asked me was what color I was. The next thing she asked me was if I believed in God. I told her "Yes, absolutely." And I said that I felt God had a hand in why I was on the phone with her that very minute. Then she asked if I lived a Christian lifestyle and I said yes. I promised her that I would teach her little girl to be kind and generous. I would teach her that she was a daughter of God, and I would teach her to work and serve others. I told the birth mother that I would love her daughter more than life itself.

Then she wanted to talk with Matt alone. I don't exactly know what they talked about, but the tears pretty much explained everything. They had a very spiritual conversation. About fifteen minutes after we hung up with her, the agency called and said that the birth mother had called to tell them that we were the family she had been waiting for and that she wanted us to be the parents of her little girl. We were overjoyed and scared to death. I had spoken with the agency on Thursday. On Friday the adoption was put together, and on Saturday at 4 AM, we left to go pick up our little girl. When we called our caseworker through LDSFS, he said he had never seen an adoption put together this fast. We had only been approved nine days when we got that first phone call from my aunt.

Now I know why I felt so much urgency. When we got to Las Vegas and saw our little Sophie for the first time, she was so tiny. At five weeks she was still only five pounds. It seemed like a miracle that this beautiful little girl was really our child. Matt was the proudest dad ever. He and Sophie had an instant connection. She was so at peace in his arms, and I knew Heavenly Father had brought us together as a forever family.

Since then I have also adopted a little white baby girl, and when I sent my profile to her birth mother, she said she picked our family because of our little black girl. She wanted her baby to grow up with a family that was color blind. I love this story because I can tell Sophie that we got Emmy because of her. Heavenly Father has a plan for every family. I love the plan he had for me.

16

MATT & MARTHA'S STORY

Get on your knees and ask for the blessings of the Lord; then stand on your feet and do what you are asked to do. Then leave the matter in the hands of the Lord. You will discover that you have accomplished something beyond price.

—*Gordon B. Hinckley*[17]

Our adoption story began many years ago when I was a small girl. I remember feeling a connection with adoption that I could not understand. Every time I came in contact with couples who had adopted, I wanted to know all about their story. I felt a kinship with adoption as if I were meant to do it myself.

Later on in my teenage years, I found out I had a condition that would make it difficult if not impossible to have children of my own. This knowledge was difficult to hear, but I was comforted with the knowledge that someday I would adopt. I met my sweetheart in an institute class after his mission. We became dear friends, and then our friendship grew into a deep love. After our marriage we began the trying process of infertility treatments. After trying many attempts, we were finally able to have a child. Our son was born nine weeks early. He was 3 lbs. and 16½ inches long. He was in the NICU for six weeks.

He is such a miracle! He and I both almost lost our lives, but the Lord blessed us, and now we are both healthy.

When our son was fifteen months old, my condition became worse, and I needed to have a hysterectomy. I had prayed and knew that this was the right course of action for our family, but I didn't want to accept it. After months of fighting the inspiration I had received, I accepted the fact that I would no longer be able to bear children. This was a very stressful time for our family. Our son's medical bills were extremely expensive, and my husband had just lost his job. Now I was facing a hysterectomy. I felt as if the Lord was kicking us when we were down.

I remembered someone saying we needed to praise God through our trials. We had to thank him for what we had. I didn't feel very grateful; I only wanted to pity myself. After weeks of prayer and fasting, I began to pray with gratitude for the things I had. I had a husband who loved me and a son who was healthy, and I had the gospel. My attitude slowly changed, and I began to look forward to my impending surgery with faith instead of fear.

I went to the hospital the day before my surgery for a pre-op. I remember feeling numb inside as I walked back to the car. It was raining, and I felt like the weather outside matched my feelings. I sat in the car, listening to the rain pound the windshield, and I prayed. I prayed for our lives, for our situation. I told God that I was following the inspiration I had been given. I told him it was hard for me and that I was scared. My husband was still without a job, we still had medical bills to pay from my son, and I was about to have surgery myself. Just as I finished my prayer, my cell phone rang. It was my husband. He told me that about ten minutes earlier he had been offered a job. As I hung up the phone, I knew that God had blessed us for going forward in faith. I knew we were on the right path.

My husband and I decided to put our papers in with LDS Family Services (LDSFS) about four months after my surgery. We knew there were more children to come to our family, and we were excited to see how they would come into our home. We went to all the classes, made our profile, and then we waited. At first we waited with excitement. Then that excitement turned to anxiety, then fear, then despair. As the weeks turned into months and as my desire to have another child grew, I felt myself sinking into darkness. About six months after we put our papers in with LDSFS, my mom had a neighbor call her. She told my mom that they had adopted and that the birth mom of their little girl was in prison and was pregnant. The birth mom wanted to place her baby for adoption, but my mom's neighbor couldn't take the baby. She asked my mom if we might want to have this baby. We were so excited! I felt like this was our blessing! We had waited and prayed—this was our baby!

A couple weeks later, the birth mom wanted to talk with us from the prison. I agreed to go to my mom's neighbor's house and talk with the birth mom on the phone. The warden would call us there, and we could talk with the birth mom. I went to my mom's neighbor's home, and we waited. An hour after the scheduled time for the phone call, I began to worry that something had gone wrong. Did the birth mom change her mind? Did she just hate me? Did she decide to keep the baby? Two hours passed, and still nothing. Then my mom's neighbor called the prison to see what was going on. The warden said that they had taken the birth mom to the doctor and had found out that the birth mom was not pregnant—she had lied. As this kind neighbor explained to me what had occurred, I tried to hold myself together. I couldn't imagine why anyone would lie about something like that. I felt as if I were dying. My heart hurt in ways I couldn't explain. As I drove home ,I cried, I screamed, and I pleaded with the Lord for answers.

As time went on, my heart started to heal. We pushed forward, knowing that we would eventually find the baby that was supposed to be in our home. Two years after we had put our adoption papers in, we decided to put our profile on a website. We thought this might help more birth moms see us.

A week after we put our profile online, we were contacted by a birth mom. Her name was Sharon (name has been changed). She explained that she was LDS, and she lived in Colorado. She was in college and had become pregnant. She asked us why were hoping to adopt, and she asked about our family. We emailed her more about us. Sharon emailed us back and forth for weeks. Then she started emailing us three and four times a day. I felt so connected to her! We had so many things in common. She told us that she liked us and wanted us to have her baby. I knew that this was it—here was the answer to my prayers. We exchanged phone numbers with Sharon, and one day while I was folding laundry she called. I was scared to death to talk with her! I didn't know what I was going to say. As I talked with her I remember thinking, *I am talking with the birth mom of my child!*

Sharon contacted us again and said that she and her family were coming to Utah to see some family and that she wanted to meet us. We were thrilled! We decided on a day and a time to meet. Sharon said she would call us an hour before we were supposed to meet and tell us what restaurant her family had decided to go to. The day arrived, and I got myself ready and changed my clothes five times. I sat on the couch in our family room and set the phone next to me and waited. The time came when she was supposed to call, and then the time passed. One, two, three, four hours passed. I still sat with the phone next to me. I was sure she had gotten sick, or that they'd had car trouble and they would call.

We never heard from Sharon again. I sent her emails asking if she was okay, if anything had happened. I never got a response. Once again I couldn't understand why anyone would do that. I told God that I couldn't take it anymore; my heart could only be broken so many times.

One day as I was talking with my mom, I told her that it wasn't fair. We couldn't afford to go to another agency other than LDSFS, and I didn't think my ability to be a mother should be based solely on my ability to pay for it. I felt as if I were between a rock and a hard place. I had no idea how God would get a child to our home. It was impossible. My mom reminded me of the story of Moses and the children of Israel. When Moses had freed the Israelites from slavery, they had camped by the Red Sea. Pharaoh's army had come for them, and they were trapped between the army and the sea. My mother said she was sure many of the Israelites were upset thinking, "Thanks, Moses! You free us, and now we have only two choices of how we want to die—the army or drowning!" For the Israelites, the situation was impossible, but my mom told me it only looked impossible if you didn't put God into the equation. As we all remember, Moses was told to stretch forth his hands, and God parted the Red Sea and the Israelites walked through on dry ground. My mom told me that God would part the Red Sea in my life. I just had to believe he would.

Several months later, we decided to take our son swimming. At the pool we ran into one of the couples that had been in our adoption classes several years before. They had adopted a beautiful baby, and we talked with them and discussed how they were able to adopt. As we talked, I had an overwhelming feeling that my baby was coming. I went to the temple by myself, fasting and praying. As I sat in the celestial room, I let all my fears, anxiety, anger, and doubt wash away. I wept in the celestial room for a long time. I needed to put all my feelings at the feet of my Heavenly Father. After that my husband and I both knew that we needed to find our baby. I can't really explain all the emotions that I had or how it all happened, but all of a sudden inspiration started coming in waves. I knew that our baby was a girl, I knew she was African-American, and I knew she would come to us from Heart and Soul Adoptions.

We refinanced our home to pay for the new agency fees. It was a scary time for us. We didn't want to make an unwise financial decision, but we knew that our baby was coming from the agency and fast. Once we decided to refinance, everything started to fall apart—we knew we were on the right track because we were coming up against serious opposition. The bank lost our papers twice, and then the bank was robbed the day we were supposed to sign papers. Our car broke down, our tires blew out, our washing machine died, and our dishwasher also quit working. The stress was at times almost more than I could handle.

Through it all, there was a peace that we knew we were making the right decision. We finally signed the papers for the refinance and handed in all our paperwork to the adoption agency. The next day my husband was called into his boss's office. His boss told him that they were looking at their employees' salaries, and my husband's was a little lower than they had thought, so they were giving him a raise. The raise went into effect the day our first payment on the house was due. What a blessing! Someone we knew had a dishwasher that they didn't need that still worked, and they gave it to us. Then one day our washing machine just started working again. Everything was looking up.

One Sunday we went to church and as I was sitting in sacrament meeting, I realized that I had forgotten to take some medication for my condition. My husband went home to get it. When he arrived back at church, he told us we needed to go home because our caseworker from Heart and Soul Adoptions had called. We called her back, and she informed us that a birth mom had chosen us, and she was due any day! The birth mom's name was Erin. Erin was having a girl, and she was African-American.

Two weeks later, we had gone to buy some shoes at the store. While I was at the cash register, my cell phone rang. It was our caseworker. She informed me that Erin had delivered a healthy baby girl. I started screaming and crying, and the cashier looked at me like I had lost my mind. I started asking questions about how much she weighed, what she looked like, and how Erin was doing. When I hung up the phone, I announced to the cashier that I had just had a baby! When I realized that must not have made sense to her I explained that we were adopting and the birth mom had just had the baby. Then both the cashier and I were crying. Matt and I spent that entire evening calling all our family and friends.

Due to some complications with the birth father, Erin flew here to Utah to sign the adoption papers. We were to meet her at the social worker's home on December 14, which was also our five-year anniversary. I was sick all day; my stomach was in knots. I didn't know what to say to Erin or how to express my gratitude. How could I thank someone for giving me the most precious and beautiful gift in the world? How can you thank someone for doing something for you that you can't do for yourself? As we pulled up to the social worker's home, I was shaking. I could see Erin holding a baby through the window in the door. When I walked in, I said hello to Erin and asked how she was. Then Erin asked me if I wanted to hold my baby. As I took our daughter Ella in my arms, a strange thing happened. I knew who she was. I had felt this child's spirit before.

Through our entire adoption process, the thing that kept me going was that I felt a spirit of the child that was to come to our home. I could feel her, and I knew I had to find her. I recognized Ella's spirit as the child I had always felt with me. I was also amazed at how incredibly gorgeous she was—and still is. She was the most perfect baby girl! We then signed the adoption papers. Erin had to go back to the airport shortly, and we asked her if she wanted to get something to eat before she left. She said she wanted to go to IHOP. We took her there, and we sat together, trading off holding Ella. Erin told us about herself and her dreams and aspirations. It was a peaceful, easy, and wonderful time. Then the caseworker told us that Erin had to go. Erin turned to me and asked if she could hold Ella one last time. I started to cry. I watched as this young girl whispered in her daughter's ear. She kissed Ella and handed her back to me. We hugged and both started to sob.

Erin thanked me for taking Ella so that she could go to school and get an education. I told her that she never needed to thank me; she was giving me the most precious gift, and I would always be in her debt. We held each other for a long time. Then Erin got up and left. Watching Erin leave was the hardest thing I have ever done. I cried the whole way home.

Ella is such a ray of sunshine in our family. She is my daughter. I feel the exact same way about her as if I had given birth to her myself. Heavenly Father parted the Red Sea in our lives so we could get Ella into our family. I learned two things from this experience of adopting. First, that motherhood is not bearing children, it is bearing with them. It is the love you have for them, the nurture, the caring that makes you their mother. It is not biology—it is love. Second, I learned that if God had moved that many mountains for us to get Ella into our home—just one child, in one home, out of billions of people on the earth—how much do you think God cares for each one of us? I know that Heavenly Father has a plan for each of us. I know he knows us and cares for us individually. Heavenly Father can and will part any sea, move any mountain, and clear any path. He makes the impossible possible.

Ruby Guymon
photo by Ember Murdoch

Helpful Information

The Lord gives compensating blessings to those who sacrifice their will to His. Speaking messianically, the prophet Isaiah proclaimed, "the Lord hath anointed me . . . to give . . . beauty for ashes, the oil of joy for mourning, the garment of praise for the spirit of heaviness" (Isaiah 61:1, 3).

—*Rebecca M. Taylor*[18]

I know I could list all of the wonderful adoption agencies that everyone has gone through, but I know some people would be upset if certain agencies were left off the list, or someone might get upset because they had a bad experience with a suggested adoption agency. So my best advice to anyone who would like to adopt transracially would be to do a little investigating. Talk to people who have adopted. Talk to as many people as you can—the more, the better. Ask as many questions as you can think of. Start right now by making a list of questions you have. If you go straight to the adoption agencies, always ask for referrals, and then follow up on them. This is one of the most important decisions of your life, so spending time on this part of it will save you heartache, money, and wasted time.

My second bit of advice, once you've prayerfully made the decision to adopt a child of a different race, is to network. Find other families like yours. A good tool is the Internet. I found a great Yahoo! chat group for transracial families in my area and have met some wonderful women, who have been very generous with their wisdom.

There are also great forums on the Internet for white parents of black children. These resources will guide you and lead you to the answers you need. As a white parent, I didn't have the experience or knowledge to deal with the hair and skin of my black children, so I did my research. You might feel like you're taking college courses on how to raise a black child, and that's okay. Just make sure you learn as much as you can. Your child deserves it. The hair and skin of black children are different and need to be treated differently. It is a lot of work and takes a lot time, but it is a work of love, and your love for and closeness with your child will grow from this service.

With that being said, my final bit of advice is this: love your child. Know that your child is a gift from God and that even though hard times will come, and you will have to deal with situations that are difficult, Heavenly Father knew you were up to the task. Racism isn't dead. But let's stomp on it as much as we can. Loving and raising these beautiful children is the best example we can show to the world that God is no respecter of persons. God loves each and every one of us the same. Let's follow his example.

Some Helpful Websites:

- www.tolerance.org
- www.nysccc.org/trarts/trarts (transracial adoption articles)
- www.ldsgenesisgroup.org (A ward where black members of the Church, and white families who have adopted black children, can come together.)

SOURCES

1. David A. Bednar "The Tender Mercies of the Lord," *Ensign*, May 2005, 99.

2. Spencer W. Kimball, "There Is Purpose in Life," *New Era*, Sept. 1974, 4.

3. See "The Family: A Proclamation to the World," *Ensign*, Nov. 1995, 102.

4. James E. Faust, "How Near to the Angels," *Ensign*, May 1998, 95.

5. Bonnie D. Parkin, "Finding Faith in Every Footstep," *Ensign*, May 1997, 84; including quote by Boyd K. Packer as found in Lucile C. Tate, *Boyd K. Packer: A Watchman on the Tower* (Salt Lake City: Bookcraft, 1995), 138.

6. Graham W. Doxey, "The Voice Is Still Small," *Ensign*, Nov. 1991, 25.

7. Richard G. Scott, "Finding Joy in Life," *Ensign*, May 1996, 24.

8. Spencer W. Kimball, "The Role of Righteous Women," *Ensign*, Nov. 1979, 102.

9. Thomas S. Monson, "The Spirit of Relief Society," *Ensign*, May 1992, 100.

10. Henry B. Eyring, "To Draw Closer to God," *Ensign*, May 1991, 65.

11. Neal A. Maxwell, "'Becometh As a Child'," *Ensign*, May 1996, 68.

12. Richard G. Scott, "Using the Supernal Gift of Prayer," *Ensign*, May 2007, 8–11.

13. Rebecca M. Taylor, "Why Adoption?," *Ensign*, Jan. 2008, 46–52.

14. First Presidency statement, Oct. 4, 2006, as quoted in Taylor, "Why Adoption?".

15. Boyd K. Packer, "A Defense and a Refuge," *Ensign*, Nov. 2006, 85–88.

16. Joseph Smith, as recorded in *History of the Church,* vol. 4, second revised edition (Salt Lake City: Deseret Book, 1976), 605; from a discourse given by Joseph Smith on Apr. 28, 1842, in Nauvoo, Illinois; reported by Eliza R. Snow.

17. Gordon B. Hinckley, "To the Women of the Church," *Ensign*, Nov. 2003, 113.

18. Taylor, "Why Adoption?"

About the Author

Shannon Guymon lives in Utah with her husband and six children. In what little free time she can find, she enjoys being in the mountains, gardening, traveling, spending time with her family, and, of course, writing.

In addition to *Child of Many Colors*, Shannon is the author of *Never Letting Go of Hope*, *A Trusting Heart*, *Justifiable Means*, *Forever Friends*, *Soul Searching*, *Makeover*, and *Taking Chances*.

photo by Kathy Tenney